I0024439

John Henry Oerter

The Social Question in the Light of History and the Word of Truth

John Henry Oerter

The Social Question in the Light of History and the Word of Truth

ISBN/EAN: 9783337270025

Printed in Europe, USA, Canada, Australia, Japan

Cover: Foto ©Lupo / pixelio.de

More available books at **www.hansebooks.com**

THE

SOCIAL QUESTION

IN THE

LIGHT OF HISTORY AND THE

WORD OF TRUTH.

— B Y —

REV. JOHN H. OERTER, D. D.

NEW YORK :

E. GLAESER.

NEW YORK BOOK DEPOSITORY.

1887.

DODD & REED,

COMPOSITION AND ELECTROTYPING,

49 LAFAYETTE PLACE,

NEW YORK.

PREFACE.

THE following Lectures were delivered in the month of March, 1887, under the provision of the "Vedder Lectureship" of the Ref. Church in America. It was at the special suggestion of the Faculty of the Theol. Seminary at New Brunswick that the "Social Question" was made the subject of the five discourses. The author does not in the least pretend to have furnished an exhaustive exposition of a theme which has assumed the position of one of the most intricate problems of the day. These Lectures merely intend to give an outline of the development of this vexed subject.

Among the numerous publications on the social question the author confesses his great indebtedness especially to the following as the most prominent:

STOEKER, A., Die Bibel und die sociale Frage.

KUEBEL, F. E., Die sociale und volkswirthschaftliche Gesetzgebung des Alten Testamentes.

CONTZEN, H., Geschichte der soc. Frage.

LANGE, F. A., Die Arbeiterfrage.

SCHOENBERG, G., Die ethisch-relig. Bedeutung der soc. Frage.

RATZINGER, G., Die Volkswirthschaft in ihren sittlichen Grundlagen.

KUNTZE, J. E., Die soc. Frage und die innere Mission.

HAEPE, G., Dr. jur, Die Socialreform und die innere Mission.

HELD, A., Zwei Buecher zur soc. Geschichte Englands.

WAGNER, A., Lehrbuch, etc., Die Grundlage.

SCHOENBERG, G., Handbuch der polit. Oconomie.

ROSCHER, W., Ansichten der Volkswirthschaft. 2 vols.

ROSCHER, W., Grundlagen der Nationaloekonomie.

RESCH, P., Entwickelungsstufen der Volkswirthschaft.

SCHAEFFLE, A. E. FR., Bau und Leben des soc. Koerpers. 3 vols.

IHERING, R. v., Der Zweck im Recht. 2 vols.

ARNOLD, W., Cultur und Rechtsleben.

ARNOLD, W., Cultur und Recht der Roemer.

HOLLENBERG, W., Die soc. Gesetzgebung.

THIERSCH, H. J., Ueber den christlichen Staat.

MENGER, A., Das Recht auf den vollen Arbeitsertrag.

SCHEEL, H. v., Eigenthum und Erbrecht.

SCHIPPEL, M., Staatliche Lohnregulirung.

SCHIPPEL, M., Modernes Elend.

ROESSLER, H., Ueber die Grundlehren der Volkswirthschaftslehre Adam Smith.

HELD, A., Socialismus, Social Demokratie u. Social Politik.

SCHAEFFLE, Quintessenz des Socialismus

SCHAEFFLE, Ausichtslosigkeit, etc.

MARTENSEN, H., Socialismus u. Christenthum.

SCHRAMM, C. A., Rodbertus, Marx, Lasalle.

ZACHER, Die Rothe Internationale.

MEYER, R., Der Emancipationskampf des 4. Standes.

OERTER, J. H., Der Socialismus der Gegenwart.

JOH. H. OERTER.

CONTENTS.

LECTURE I.

THE SOCIAL QUESTION IN THE OLD AND THE NEW TESTAMENT, AND DURING THE VARIOUS TIMES OF SERVITUDE.

" The Social Question in the Light of History and the Word of Truth," will be the subject of the " Vedder Lectures " this year. Before entering, however, upon this vexing theme, allow me to preface the same by a few explanatory remarks, in order to justify the selection of such a topic.

The Social Question is in fact co-existing with the formation of society itself. For at all times in history, we notice among men the contrast between rich and poor, and consequently a vehement opposition against too great an economic difference. But never before has this opposition assumed such a progressively revolutionary attitude as in our own day. The reason for this is found in the fact that at present, " The actual inequality of possessions, is regarded by the great mass as standing in direct opposition to the generally acknowledged equality of individual rights of all men." Hence the weak and poor rise, even revolt, against the division of property, as it has been formed by various processes of times past.

But even this alarming attitude of the Social Question, would hardly justify me in making this difficult and perplexing problem the object of our consideration, if it presented merely a material and economic aspect. Should it be true, what political economy and the laboring classes in general maintain, that it amounts to nothing more than a question of wages or of a better distribution of the national income, then the provisions under which these lectures are held, would exclude a discussion like the one proposed.

But I am confident of being able to show the pre-eminently *moral and religious* character of a movement which agitates the whole civilized world, by proving that most of the present social and economic evils are but the natural outgrowth of irreligious principles underlying political economy and social orders. To do this, it will be necessary first of all to take a brief survey of the historic developement of the Social Question, and at the same time to test the results of the same, by that never failing standard which the Word of Eternal Truth furnishes us.

By that, we will be enabled to form a true conception

of the actual state and character of the Social Question, which I consider of primary importance for a correct and successful solution of this intricate problem. Society in general must come to a clear understanding of the real causes of the present trouble ; if they are ever to be removed.

The following presentations do not in the least assume to be an exhaustive exposition of a subject, which has challenged the minds of men who have devoted their entire attention to the study of the Social Question and its solution. They merely intend to throw, if possible, some light on a perplexing subject, and to suggest for your consideration a few points that might be serviceable to its final solution. The remainder of the present lecture will be devoted to an effort, to secure to us a firm stand-point, by establishing the economic principles of the Old and New Testaments. ·By way of contrast, then, we will glance at the nature of the Social Problem during the different Times of Servitude.

In the Old Testament the ideas of State, Church and Society essentially coincide. Hence its social and economic regulations must be considered in connection with its civil and religious enactments.

Now, the Jewish commonwealth was not an accidental product of historical events, or a conglomeration of heter-- ogeneous fragments of conquered nations, with, perhaps,

an original race forming the governing element. It was
rather the natural outgrowth of a pure lineage or descent.
But it is not this consanguinity, which in the eyes of the
Law, elevates Israel to the rank and authority of a nation,
but a specific act of Divine election, that gives to it national existence. "Is not he (Jehovah) thy Father, that
bought thee? hath He not made thee and established
thee?" [Deut. xxxii: 6, 18.] The deliverance out of the
house of bondage, the giving of the Law on Mount Sinai,
and the leading into the land of Canaan, appear as the
three marked acts of Divine grace, by means of which the
chosen people of God were made a distinct and peculiar
nation. [See Deut. xv: 15; xxxii: 16; Lev. 25:38.] The
purpose of this election is expressed in the words of Jehovah: "Ye shall be unto me a kingdom of priests, and
a holy nation," [Exod. xix: 6.] Israel was pre-eminently
God's chosen people, and to this law of his purpose, all
the civil, political and economic rules, regulations and
divisions, were made subservient. Keeping this in mind
we can understand why the Supreme Law-giver threw
such a safeguard around his people, in order to keep them
untarnished by the pollutions of the surrounding pagan
nations; why so many ordinances tended towards the
preservation of the natural divisions into tribes, families,
and households, [Josh. vii: 14, 17, 18]; and why aside
from these organic demarcations, the Old Testament did

not, and would not, recognize any distinction on account of birth or inheritance. Jewish history knows nothing of nobility or preference on account of descent, no feudal power or dependency. "Israel is a people of brothers, because it is a people of servants of God." This fact will also help us amazingly to understand the *economic* provisions made by the law of God. We will first direct our attention to the Old Testament idea of *property*, that essential and universal factor of production.

Israel being designed for a farming people, the Land of Canaan was given to it for its possession. But just, as well as it had to consider its national existence as the result of a special act of God's sovereignty ; so the law required it, to look upon the land as a peculiar gift of Jehovah. All the agrarian provisions are based on the fundamental principle and declaration of the Supreme Law-giver : "The land is mine ; for ye are strangers and sojourners with me." Lev. xxv: 23. In Egypt the King, as the incarnation of the Godhead, was discretionary possessor of the entire country ; but among the chosen people Jehovah himself was to be considered, as the absolute sovereign and rightful owner of the promised land. Although the twelve tribes, at the point of the sword, had to conquer every inch of the land of Canaan, yet according to the law they could only lay the claim as tenants of Jehovah to it. Each tribe had its allotted portion

not by fee simple, but in trust, that is, it possessed
the right of turning to use and advantage, but not the
right of disposal.

This position of the law was of great consequence in
more than one respect. Israel could under no circum-
stance sell the land, neither collectively nor individually.
Besides, it had to learn the important lesson, that the
prosperity of the land stood in close connection with the
behavior of the people towards the law of *Jehovah*. Yea,
it was made the chief condition of the tenancy, that in
the case of obedience to the law, the soil would always
yield plentifully, while on the other hand, disobedience
would bring poverty upon the people, and finally become
the cause of forcible dispossession, [Deut. xxviii; Lev. xxvi].
National wealth, therefore, was not to be considered in
Israel as the result of the energy of the people; but as a
free gift of God, dependent, however, on the religious
life of the nation. Strictly speaking the Old Testament
law never considers a mere possession, or the proceeds
thereof, or from labor rendered as property; the latter invariably appears as a benefaction of the God of Israel.
Hence we do not hear anything of an absolute right of
man to any earthly possession, that right according to
Scripture, belongs exclusively to the Disposer of all
things.

It is true, the land of Canaan was given to Israel, as a

possession of its own ; but that only relatively and with regard to the surrounding nations. Otherwise Jehovah remained forever the chief owner. Aside from this proviso, Israel in its totality held the title to the promised inheritance ; not that the management thereof, should be in the hands of the entire commonwealth. On the contrary the law expressly demanded the distribution of the land in the order and manner of the natural divisions of the tribes, families, and households, each of which received a distinct allotted estate in fee, which it held as an inalienable and hereditary property; [Numb.xxvi: 53–55 ; xxxiii: 54]. That is, to say, the Old Testament law established *private property*, and was very anxious to keep, if possible, each individual possession intact. For example, the injunction respecting the marriage of the daughter of Zelophehad [Numb. xxvii: 4-7], the well-known institution of the kinsman [Lev. xxv: 24, 26], the provisions made with reference to the redemption of sold property, at any time [Lev. xxv], and especially the requirements concerning the restitution of all alienated property in the year of Jubilee: everything was calculated to preserve to the original owners, whether tribe, or family, or household, that portion which was allotted to them by the will of Jehovah.

The same wise and benign circumspection is noticed, when we look at the provisions made with regard to the

unavoidable social difference of *rich and poor*. According to Deut. xv: 4, 5, the economic aim and end of the
theocratic life of Israel was the prevention of poverty.
But as that depended on a strict and general observance
of the law, Jehovah knew but too well, that even among
his chosen people there would be continually needy persons [ver. 11]. But in order to prevent a too great a
gulf among the members of the Theocracy, the Supreme
Law-giver issued such regulations, that on the one side
would check the accumulation of enormous wealth, guard
against impoverishment on the other ; and would, also,
throw obstacles in the way of overreaching on the part of
the rich. Thus, for example, the laws respecting redemption, and final restitution of property, in the year of
Jubilee, besides achieving the direct purposes mentioned
before, were also intended as a restraint on human avariciousness. Besides, the fact that usury and taking interest of any member of the covenant people, was strictly
forbidden, made all speculations in exchange, etc., impossible. There was no chance for a few to gather up the
possessions in the land, or to enrich themselves out of
the vicissitudes of life, or the reverses of their fellowmen;
unless they trampled under foot the explicit statutes of
the Divine law. That such was done, is evident from the
rebuke of the prophets; [Isa. v: 8; Mic. ii: 2:] "Woe
unto them that join house to house, that lay field to field,

till there be no place, that they may be placed alone in the midst of the earth :" and, "That oppress even a man and his heritage." But such acts of avidity were known to stand in open violation of the theocratic code of laws; they were by no means shielded by it.

The same eagerness is manifested with reference to the prevention of *poverty*. During the time of harvest, the poor enjoyed the privilege of gathering up what was commanded to be left for them on the fields. [Deut. xxiii: 24 et seq.; Lev. xix: 10; xxiii: 22.] Especially in the year of tithing (the third) the second tenth was to be given to "the stranger, the fatherless and the widow." Lastly, in the Sabbath and Jubilee years the same right was granted to the poor as to the rich, indiscriminately to apply to their daily wants, whatever the Lord in his mercy had permitted to grow. Add to these, the regulations of the law respecting *loans*, *security*, and *pawning*, etc. [Exod. xxii: 25 et seq.; Deut. xxiv: 10-13; xxv: 1-10.;] and we find a legal bulwark thrown around a helpless class, intended to protect it against the so easily aroused rapacity of the rich.

A further proof of that is found in the position, which the Old Testament law occupies with reference to *labor and laborers*. The former appears first of all as a part of the *curse* pronounced upon sin, [Gen. iii: 19]. But in the Ten Words it receives the form of a *commandment*, of an expression of the will of God for the present living, [Exod. xx: 6, Deut. v: 13; Exod. xxxv: 2]. This is the leading idea of labor throughout the Old Testament, everywhere it appears as an obligation resting upon the members of the covenant. Hence obedience to God is to form the principal motive for working; all other considerations, as that of its necessity for existence, its blessing for mankind, its compensation, are to be of secondary importance with those, that are governed by the law of Jehovah. In close connection with this stands the other truth, that everywhere in the Old Testament the result of labor,—the *product* or its *compensation—wages,*—is not chiefly and mainly considered as the necessary consequence of human exertion or work spent ; but primarily stands in the relation of an effect to a superhuman cause, namely, to the *blessing* of the Supreme Lawgiver, warranted in all cases of obedience to the law. " Your strength shall be spent in vain: for your land shall not yield her increase, neither the trees of the land yield their fruits," [Lev. xxvi: 20], says Jehovah. That is, as has been well said: "God's national economy works with fundamental factors, that are entirely different from those of modern science." [Kuebel, p. 70.]

Of the same peculiar character is the Old Testament conception of the *laborer.* The idea of labor as a Divine injunction of necessity, stamped every member of the

Jewish commonwealth as a workman. Hence the law did not create or establish, strictly speaking, any of those social distinctions known, as *employers* and *employed*, *capitalists* and *laborers*, laborless income and proceeds from toil, etc. But on account of the universal sinfulness of man it anticipated such economic differences, and it was only with reference to this anticipated state of affairs,that it made provisions for their amelioration. All Israelites are the *servants* of Jehovah; hence they are *brothers* in their relations to each other. But for the reason stated pauperization even among a nation of brothers could not be prevented. Various causes could reduce any member of the covenant-people to such a state of want, as to compel him to offer his time and strength for the services of another, in this case he became a *hired servant*. [Lev. xix: 13]. Or, he might wax so poor, that he would *even sell* himself for a limited or an unlimited time to his fellowmen, or to a stranger, [Lev. xxv : 39 et seq.; Exod. xxi: 5:6; Deut. xv: 16], and thus become a *free-will bond-servant*; or he might even be born into a state of dependence. [Exod. xxi: 3 et seq]. All these various economic conditions the law foresaw ; and it at once threw its preventing and protecting arms around those, that thus might become dependent. By a number of provisions and restrictions it reduced the actual cases of servitude to the smallest number. Bonded service could never become a degraded, established institution in Israel, as the sale of any member of the Theocracy, for the purpose of making him a bond-servant, was strictly prohibited. And in all cases of free-will servitude, the privilege of redemption by relatives or friends was granted, or the liberation demanded in the year of Jubilee. The laborer in Israel under all circumstances of life was to be considered, as a member of the Theocracy, as a brother. Hence he enjoyed in his time the rare privilege of a legal status, which was denied to the slaves of the surrounding nations. By industry and faithfulness he was permitted to put himself into the possession of personal property, a right that was not denied even to the *slave* in Israel. His work, as well as his person, was esteemed so highly in the eyes of the law, that it guaranteed to him, just as well as to his master, the blessing of the weekly Sabbath-rest; besides the social, economical privileges of the Sabbath and Jubilee-years, a humane provision, which was extended even to the laborer out of the animal kingdom. [Lev. xxv: 6, 7.]

In regard to his *wages*, it is true, the Mosaic law fixes no standard, or scale by which in each case, its limits might have been decided ; it leaves that to the mutual agreement of the parties concerned. In order, however, to protect the wage-earner against oppression, the employer is earnestly admonished not to over-reach, and it is strictly enjoined upon him to pay off his laborer every day : " Thou shalt not oppress an hired servant, that is poor and needy, whether he be of thy brethren, or of thy strangers that are in thy land within thy gates : at his day thou shalt give him his hire, neither shall the sun go down upon it; for he is poor, and setteth his heart upon it: lest he cry out against thee unto the Lord, and it be a sin unto thee." [Deut. xxiv: 14, 15; Lev. xix: 13.] On the basis and strength of this divine precept, Jeremiah, the prophet, severely denounces the transgressors thereof in the following cutting words: "Woe unto him that buildeth his house by unrighteousness, and his chambers by wrong; that useth his neighbor's service without wages, and giveth him not for his work." [Jer. xxii: 13.]

Thus a golden thread of foresight and tender care, for the poor and the needy, the dependent and serving, the serf and the slave, runs through the entire Mosaic legislation, making social disruptions, and antagonistic class-differences impossible, as long as the majesty of the law was acknowledged. The Jewish commonwealth enjoyed the rare blessing of being preserved from those social convulsions, that frequently shook the very foundation of the highly cultured states of classical renown, and finally brought them to ruin. But when with a change of industrial relations Israel forgot its God, then poverty as a morbid state of the economical life of the people appears in the foreground in a disquieting measure, and with it that social tension, which everywhere results from too great a difference in the economical status of the component parts of society.

The New Testament and the Social Question.

According to a word of Christ concerning his relation to the Old Testament law, we are fully justified in saying that it is not the purpose of Christianity to destroy that law, but rather, to make a beginning with an earnest, conscientious fulfilling of the same. But in this noble and high calling it intends not only, to serve the chosen covenant-people, a Jewish particularism, but all people under whatever condition of life it might find them. The obtaining of this end, it does not expect from any sharpening of the letter of the law, or by any aggravation of its penalties; but rather from the imparting of the renewing and reforming power of that love, which became flesh in Christ Jesus. That is, it is not the purpose of Christianity externally, by the power of laws or the authority of the State to make human affairs and circumstances conform to the Divine ideal. On the contrary, its endeavor is to regulate, penetrate, and sanctify from within all human relations, so that they may be brought into harmony with the spirit of Divine love, as it manifested itself in Christ Jesus.

On account of this peculiar, exceptional position of the New Testament, very evidently we cannot expect to find on its pages a specific *Christian-economical* legislation, nor an express doctrine concerning questions of political economy. The gospel of Christ recognizes the social and civil conditions of the different nations, just as it meets them; but it also uses every effort to fill them with its Godlike spirit, and thus to bring them into consonance with the Divine will and pleasure. For example, any attempt to construe out of passages of the New Testament a specific Christian idea of *property*, will always fail. But when already in the Old Testament, the covenant member appears as the mere tenant of Jehovah, then in the New Testament the believer is still more set forth, as the steward of his master. Here, even more than there, every external, physical, earthly possession is traced back to the Giver of all good and perfect gifts; and the use thereof made subordinate entirely and exclusively to the promotion of the honor and glory of God, to the advancement of his kingdom, and to the furtherance of the welfare of our fellowmen, as well as our own. Innumerable passages sustain this assertion.

In like manner the New Testament does not touch the external differences between rich and poor, master and servant, employer and employee. Nay, it predicts even the continuation of such relations of dependence, during

the present order of things. But at the same time it demands of all believers, that by the spirit of love and communion with Christ, all these conditions should be regulated and sanctified in such a manner, that in heart and
mind, and before God every distinction would actually be
abolished; and thus also the outside of such relations
lose every severity and hardship. Read for example,
Eph. vi.; Phil.; 1. Cor. xii.; 2. Cor. xiii.; and other like
passages, and then put the question to yourselves,
whether you can even imagine a *Christian* slaveholder,
who in the treatment of his slaves would place himself on
the prerogative granted to him by the *Roman* law? Or
an employer after the spirit and mind of Christ, who
could draw the very lifeblood out of his workmen? Or,
on the other hand a Christian laborer, who by means of a
revolver, dynamite and petroleum, would present and enforce his demands? Certainly not. The New Testament
most severely censures all those that profess Christ, but
hang their heart on riches, oppress the poor, or withhold
the just dues from the laborer; while it exhorts the dependent class to be patient and not to grudge one against
another. [See especially Jas. v: 1-9.]

In regard to *labor* the New Testament does not express
any opinion, as to the different value of human accom-
plishment, or as to a full equivalent for work rendered.
But the spirit of Christianity at once raises man from that

degrading position, in which, according to the conceptions
and usages of the ancient heathen world, he himself was
to be esteemed according to the higher or lower character
of his work. In the eyes of Christ and his apostles each
individual person, as a human being, and especially as an
object of redeeming love, possesses an intrinsic value,
that is not dependent on his manual or mental achievements, either separately or collectively. He has a higher,
a moral worth. Now, when he brings this to bear on his
economical pursuits, in so far that he infuses into his
work his Christian conscienciousness and fidelity, his
delight and patience, his faith and love, then he im-
parts to it a moral value, that at once removes from
labor every menial, odious stigma. In this sense: "The
scrubbing of a pious kitchen girl is just as well a service
rendered to God than the worship of his people;" as Luther
says.

Of course, this fact does not decide anything, as to the
economic value of a specific work done, nor as to the proper
amount of wages due to it. But when it admits of no
doubt, that Christianity considers man first of all in the
light of his *moral* worth, as an object of Divine love, and
demands that he be recognized as such; then it must be
admitted, that man can never be degraded below his
labor, nor can his manual work ever be separated from his
moral being, without trampling under foot the letter and

spirit of the Word of Life. That is, labor does not depreciate the laborer, neither can it be considered as a mere material rendering, but in every case, as the conscious act of a moral, responsible being. Two things follow from this: If the workman gives himself up to idleness, he neglects his Christian duty; if the employer over-reaches those employed by him, he both materially and morally injuries them. Even where the civic law secures to proprietors certain rights as to personal obligations and services of those dependent on them; the Christian owner is exhorted to consider his claims in the light of the higher Divine law of love. Paul expects from the professing Philemon, that he would no longer regard the converted Onesimus after the civic relation of slave-right; but treat him in the spirit of Christian brotherhood. It is true, we are not justified to infer from this, that in the business relations of life, Christian consideration ought to form the rule for every scale of wages; but it certainly does follow from explicit expressions of the New Testament, as well as from legitimate inferences to be drawn from its sense and spirit, that the mere material performances ought not to be the sole turning point on which the valuation of human labor is pending. On this, however, we have to say a little more in a subsequent lecture.

The focal point of the Social problem in all ages, has always been the question, as to the just and proper distribution of the clear profit of labor, or of the national income. Now, the New Testament preaches, neither a social equality, nor an economic communism. The opposite cannot be deduced from that entirely voluntary disposal of goods, as it is noticed in the primitive church in Jerusalem. For we have here, neither an Apostolic ordering, nor a usage that extended beyond the limits of this single congregation. On the contrary, it was merely a local and temporary impulse of a powerfully moving brotherly love and communion. Nevertheless, it is evident, that New Testament Christianity is eagerly endeavoring by word and deed to equalize, as much as possible, those oppressive differences that for various reasons, might manifest themselves in the social life of its confessors. For this reason, it commands its followers in general, and the rich of this world specifically: "That they do good, that they be rich in good works, that they be ready to distribute, willing to communicate," etc. [1 Tim. vi: 17, 18; 2 Cor. ix: 8, 11]. Besides the Apostolic church laid the foundation of that *caritative* or *benevolent* system, which up to the present time has proved itself an absolutely indispensable, and highly beneficent factor in the economic life of Christian nations. It is, further, no inferior merit of the New Testament that besides fostering a spirit of general and special benevolence, it also tries to inculcate on the socially oppressed, and economically needy, obedience, patience, and forbearance. Although, the followers of Christ at the beginning were persecuted, and deprived of their earthly possession, yet nowhere in the New Testament are they incited to acts of violence or redress; but exhorted to commit their grievances to the just retribution of the coming judge. [Jas. v: 7-9.] Under the influence of the spirit of Christ attempts to murder, or social revolutionary movements are a matter of utter impossibility.

Summing up what has been said so far, it is evident that in the Old and the New Testament, especially in the latter, a solution of the Social Question is offered, that has not been surpassed by anything put forth outside of Holy Writ. Nay more, it is a fact that cannot be gainsaid, that wherever the spirit of the New Testament has penetrated the social and economical life of any community, the Social Question has never presented itself as a problem yet to be solved. But it is also well known, that Christianity, as taught and lived by Christ, his Apostles, and early followers, could not bring to bear its wholesome influence on all nations, nor even on its own confessors in every age of its existence. Hence the social problem has called forth such different attempts at its solution, that in the course of time it has developed for itself a formidable history.

The following pages purpose to outline the principal

features of that development, and to test it by the word
of Divine truth.

_____

THE SOCIAL QUESTION UNDER THE DIFFERENT FORMS OF
SERVITUDE.

The economic life of any people, is the product of
three operative factors: viz., of *private property*, or *capital;* of *labor rendered;* and the *participation in the proceeds*
of *these productive forces.* Now, history has shown beyond a doubt, that the respective share of the individual
in the national income or clear gain, always depend on
the social customs and principles of *right ;* as they exist
in a body politic with reference to property and labor.
But just here, the individual nations, and the various
periods of economic development, exhibit such a fundamental difference in the conception of these two ideas,
that the question, as to the proper share in the economic
product, assumes a variety of forms. We begin with the
Times of Servitude, that is, with those social conditions
of ages gone by, in which *personal* bondage by social or
legal forms of right was publicly recognized. In the
course of time this mode of existence has undergone various changes, or modifications, and consequently exerted
a varying influence on the distribution of the national income.

I. DURING SLAVERY.

Involuntary servitude primarily sets out in the form of complete personal restraint, that is as *slavery*. Historically, its formative causes are to be found first of all in that external power, by which the conquered and captured enemies in war were subjected to the conqueror; and that for the purpose of employing them economically for his interest. In addition to this very often unfavorable social circumstances, or subjections in consequence of oppressive need, formed another cause for slave-conditions. In every case, however, slavery has an economic basis: " For servitude,"as Wagner says,"always and everywhere can be traced back to some economical want of personal services, and of working forces in the production of goods." Hence, slavery did not arise until the primitive conditions of the hunting and fishing communities, had developed themselves gradually, into those of the *agricultural* nations. Considered in this light, slavery may be regarded as a social progress, when compared with the primary cruel custom of destroying the subdued enemy.

Now, according to *Bockh's* calculation, we find in ancient *Greece*, to begin with that country, about three-fourths of the population excluded from the benefit and protection of the law; while according to *Gibbon's* estimation, one half of the inhabitants of the *Roman* empire consisted of slaves. In consequence of these social disproportions, naturally the greatest economic inequality divided society, in these nations. Thus, for example, in *Attica*, the most civilized state of the ancient world, only 13.5 per cent. of the totality of the people possessed real estate, while in the Roman empire all riches had accumulated in the hands of the senators and the knighthood, so that the possessing portion of the population did not even amount to one-half per cent. Besides, in Greece, *labor*, as far as it produced any gain, was detested, and for that reason given over to the slave. Even an *Aristotle* could give expression to the sentence: " A good citizen ought not to concern himself with manual labor, for it blunts body and mind, and creates uncouth people." But what is still worse in the light of economic well-being, in Greece and even more so in the Roman Empire, according to law,the slave was considered and treated as a *thing*, and consequently, completely the property of his master; legally he was not a *person*. This fact explains another principle of Roman law and right, namely, that every gain, and all the earnings of the slave formed part and parcel of the property of the master. This right extended even to all the members of the slave family, and the master possessed the privilege to punish or expose these outlawed and deprived creatures, according to whim and pleasure. Of course, under such unnatural and degrading social circumstances, the economic lot of the slave was beyond description hard and miserable. It is true there have been, even in times of the greatest barbarism, noble exceptions, as is proven by the provisions of a *peculium*, or the right of the slave to a certain amount of property among other benefits. But on the whole the existence of these outcasts was wretched, as they received but enough to maintain their physical powers, and when reduced to uselessness they were put on a starvation diet.

Now, this exclusive employment of persons deprived of their liberty exerted a most disadvantageous influence on the economical developement of these classical nations; because the strong tie of mutual personal interests between master and slave was utterly wanting. In addition to this must be mentioned the sad fact, that the excessive mass of slaves, operated disastrously on the economic conditions of the free population. That is to say, the poorer class finally found it impossible to support itself, as the rich continually multiplied the number of their slaves. Thus gradually a proletariat of freemen was formed, which sunk down into a most lamentable condition, and caused Tiberius Gracchus to exclaim: "The irrational beasts possess their lair and stalls; but the warriors who fight and die for Italy, nothing but air and light, so that they with wife and children roam about unsheltered, and homeless. The address of the generals to fight *pro armis et focis* (for the honor of the arms and the fireside) sounds like mockery. The so-called lords of this world do not own a glebe, they die for the affluence and dissipation of others.'' *Mascher*, the eminent investigator of classical antiquity, very strikingly depicts its collective condition in the following words: ''In spite of all splendor and brilliancy, which dazzlingly surround classical antiquity, labor was enslaved,—the division of labor, indeed was known and its value for production prized, nevertheless production and consumption were separated in a caste-like spirit. The small number of free citizens, of mighty princes, and aristocrats, together with their philosophers, contemplated nothing else with their speculations than to allow themselves in a commodious manner to be sustained by a drove of slaves; while they themselves endeavored to pass away the time by inventions of still different extortions and acts of violence, by debauchery and ingenious enjoyments, as by well-sounding but idle conversations about the welfare of the state It is true the sages of antiquity painfully expressed it as their opinion, that labor, unorganized labor, as it then was performed, deprived man of his honor; but they were stricken with egotistic blindness, instead of ennobling labor, by imparting to it the character of the beautiful, they hunted their slaves, as they would deadly frightened beasts of the chase; and thus, they degraded them more and more. While they confessed with a wisdom becoming a statesman, that poverty destroyed the nobility of the soul, they left the acquisition of property to arbitrary exactions! They admitted that capital without labor would bear no fruit, and yet from that they drew no other conclusion, than that there must be a caste of idle capitalists, and a caste of laboring slaves."

That is to say, to the philosophers of classical Greece and Rome, the relation of master to slave appeared to be just as natural as that of husband and wife, or of parent and child. Hence, Aristotle repudiates the idea, that slavery was the product of power and compulsion, or of arbitrary laws and social regulations. Here then, we find a system that presents to us the very opposite of those economic conditions which the Old Testament by law provided, and which the New Testament endeavors to create among mankind. In other words, slavery forms the crowning seal to the sinfulness of the human race, because it utterly ignores man's relation to his Maker, to his fellowmen, as well as to himself. It is a complete reversion of the Divine purpose with man as an accountable, moral being.

Hence we do not wonder that these unnatural conditions which prevented the peaceful and wholesome development of the state, as well as of society, caused, even in benighted Greece and Rome, incessant social and political commotions. In the former, as early as 880 B. C.

Lycurgus had made the attempt to remove the principal cause of the exciting social contentions, by abolishing
the inequality of possessions, as far as it was possible,
and by declaring every child from its seventh year the
exclusive property of the state. Two hundred years later
Solon made a similar attempt by liberating the *native*
slaves, and by granting far reaching political and social
rights to the inhabitants of Athens. But neither Sparta
nor Athens could be quieted, as the evil was not touched
at its root.

In Rome the Social Question presents an uninterrupted
series of social disruptions and bloody deeds. The contest between the patricians and plebeians, grew more and
more bitter as time elapsed, until *Tiberius* and *Caius
Gracchus* arose (133 and 123 B. C.) in order to overthrow
the oligarchic party, by means of legislation and revolutionary measures, forcibly trying to put the poor and
homeless into the possession of such property, which the
rich had obtained unjustly. Both these reformers were
killed in tumults, and the attempted reforms initiated a
series of civil wars, until the conflict of the parties was
ended by an unprecedented despotism—always the beginning of the end. Under such ruinous and decomposing
political, and social conditions, the final downfall of the two
lordliest and most imperious states of antiquity, could not
be avoided. But we will pass on to the time of feudalism.

II.   DURING THE TIME OF FEUDALISM.

Christianity, as it shines forth from the pages of the
New Testament, contains so many and such vigorous
germs of vitality, that, when permitted to sprout, state, as
well as social life are enabled to develop themselves har-
moniously and satisfactorily.   Now, in the youthful Germanic world these dormant seeds, for a time, seemed to
open and to expand into full blossoms.   The natural dispositions, emotions, and social ideas of these tribes, received from Christianity, "Rich nourishment and bouy-
ancy.   In the political, scientific and social life of the
middle ages especially, the lasting efforts of Christianity
showed themselves in a zeal for a just and beneficial government, in their opposition to arbitrariness, and tyranny,
and in the great enthusiasm for the emancipation of other
social classes from the bonds of slavery."

But this powerfully moving spirit of Christianity, was
checked, on the other hand, by political factions, domes-
tic feuds, and especially by the influence of their ante-
Christian social conceptions.   In consequence thereof,
even the embracing of the Christian religion could not
prevent the formation of those unfree conditions of life,
which in their different modifications are designated by
the collective name of *feudalism*.

Slavery in the long run, did not answer all economic
wants.   The more extensively and intensely agriculture

had to be pursued, the larger the claims of the unfolding handicraft and of technics in general became, the less did slave work satisfy the economic wants of the time. Hence it died out by degress and gave room to *serfdom*.

The origin of the same cannot, as is the case with slavery, be traced back to conquests, or acts of violence; it rather finds its explanation in oppressive economical circumstances. Persons originally free became poor, lacked therefore the necessary means, or the requisite estate for independent management; or in times of juridical insecurity they were unable to protect themselves. In consequence of these and other circumstances they were compelled to give themselves over to the wealthy proprietor, or the church, as serfs or bondsmen, tied to the glebe, or to bonded-services.

We discover, therefore, in this dependent class, not the conquered of foreign nations, but for the greatest part, the economically reduced descendants of the conquerors themselves. The then so prevalent idea, that "Lording over others was for those in power, the most natural basis for drawing income," brought those without a home and the means of subsistence into such dependency. Whosoever tilled the land of another in any form, was, according to the juridical perceptions of those times, subjected also with his person to the respective owner, or in other words he became a serf. It is true, he was permitted to manage his own economy independent of that of his lord or master, and in this respect he distinguishes himself economically from the slave. But nevertheless, he was bound, either to hand over to the owner, measured or unmeasured shares, out of the proceeds of the entire cultivation of the ground, or while his master reserved for himself the best part of the land, not only to cultivate that so retained portion, but also to divide the products of his own division between himself and the proprietor, besides being compelled to furnish for the whole the necessary human or animal forces. From this thraldom the serf could never be released. Besides this, he was subjected to the disciplinary and punitive power of the owner almost without a condition, and thus he was chained to his lord and the clod in a manner, that his lot appears to be but a slight amelioration of slavery. Even the artisan, if he could not set out independently, was tied down in the same manner. And as during the middle ages the entire national economy was governed by the custom of paying off all dues in the natural products, we can easily imagine with *Lasalle*, the lively scenes, when on the appointed day the tailors, shoemakers, glovers, coopers, carpenters, smiths, etc., brought the due products of their respective art to the feudal lord.

After this severer form of serfdom had ceased to exist, we still find those *bonded-services*, which consisted in dues of natural products, or in personal labor, and which were required even of children and servants. This social form of servitude, in fact displaced the former, when the progresses in agriculture, in handicraft, and trade, but more especially, "When transition from paying off in natural products, to paying in money; when the development of cities and the greater demand of the enlarged population, concentrated therein; when further, the desire for more artful industrial, and for mental labor," (Wagner) called forth a corresponding development of the principle of *personal liberty*. Then the rude form did not answer any more the growing need, or in other words, the economic want in time changed the economic dependency.

Now, here the question arises how these unnatural feudal conditions, could ever enter Christian communities, and in the face of the liberating influence of the gospel, maintain themselves during such a long period. The answer must be sought in the fact, that from the time of the forcible conversion of the heathen tribes and nations, many a pagan custom and conception was allowed to be retained. And in this connection, it is more particularly to be observed, that the introduction of the *Roman* law and right into the social relations of the Germanic tribes mightily changed their economic conditions. For according to it, *labor* presents but the same value as the *object*

or thing. And "Just in the same manner, as by Roman
right the proprietor of the ground gets into possession of
the plant, as soon as it has taken root, by the same principles of law he also is entitled to the seed sown by
another, and the crops springing therefrom. So also in
the sphere of obligations, the Roman law constantly puts
dare, as the conveying of property in chattel, along side
with the *facere*, designating any doing or performing.
Thus the idea of labor, which, it is true, is hidden in it,
does not stand out as an independent conception, to be
appreciated separately and distinctly." (Contzen.)

Now these principles of right had penetrated the juridical perceptions of the middle ages, and for the greatest
part supplanted the Christian spirit in social legislation.
Besides popery had developed such a lordly and hierarchical spirit, that these feudal conditions were prevalent,
even inside the church and thus received a powerful support. In the state *absolutism* reigned supremely, which
on its part again "licensed, chartered, tutored, and protected mercantilism."

You will readily perceive that under such circumstances, labor suffered injury and loss; and the distribution of the national income could not, but be highly unequal. Thus, for example, in *England* according to the
statements of the so-called domesday book, we find in
the first half of the eleventh century at least three-fourths

of the population without any possession; and without that precious boon, personal liberty. The same holds true as to other countries. Add to this the fact, that the feudal lord by law possessed unlimited authority over the entire time and proceeds of the bonded servant; and that according to the decision of the anglo-normanic jurist *Bracton* in the 13th century the estate of the serf could be seized by his master,—not to mention other evils, and you must admit, that in feudalism circumstances had been developed, which were anything but Christianlike and satisfactory.

Baumstark, the historian, undoubtedly presents the same very correctly in the following words: "Feudalism and the encroaching Roman right, each separately, and in spite of their conflicting tendencies yet conjointly, promoted a system of social and civil polity which for centuries to come not only corrupted the conditions of the laboring class most disastrously, but which also bore heavily on the entire national economy, as it arrested and stunned its progress. These two in connection with papal policy, deprived the monarchical power, in whose interest the elevation of the middle and lower classes lay, of its independence and efficiency. They stamped the right of self-determination and of self-legislation of the free, as the aristocratic prerogative of a few families, without diminishing the public burdens of their liege-men. They aggra-

vated and multiplied the seigneurial and feudal exactions put
on the lower classes. They confused the ideas of the popu-
lar native right, which needed to be developed out of their
own imperfection. Add to this the indolent life of
debauchery and of adventurous nuisance of the feudal
lords, who were not satisfied with being inactive and with
impoverishing the estate; but who also endeavored to find
their entertainment and gain, in checking and robbing
commerce and trade." Certainly a sad picture of the
conditions of the laboring classes, and that not perchance
under the reign of pagan governments, but in the midst of
Christian nations, and with the cognizance, nay, even the
consent of the church of God!

It is true, counteracting influences have asserted themselves at all times. Thus as early as in the days of
Augustine, the fathers of the church organized religious
orders and societies, in order to induce the rich to deeds
of benevolence towards the poor, and to assist in times of
need and poverty. By words and writings the attention
of the possessors of earthly goods was called to the importance of their possessions, and to the great responsibility in regard to the management of the same, besides
the necessity of a Christian, affectionate treatment of the
lower classes. So also the founding of monastic orders
exerted a wholesome economic influence, until by accumulating worldly possessions and power they alas, became

themselves instrumental in aggravating the existing social misery. Even those brotherhoods that were bound by the anathema, as the *Humiliates*, the *Beghards*, and the *Beguines*, did not remain without a marked impression upon the economic and social relations of their times, as long as they did not depart from their original religious object and aim.

A special social and economical purpose was pursued by those *corporations* and *guilds*, that sprung up since the twelfth century. Their primary object, indeed, was by means of a closer union and a consolidation of mutual interests to form a counterweight against the overbearing nobility and patriciate. But aside from that they also turned their attention to the furtherance of their own economic interests. In the several cities the different branches of trade and craft formed into a separate body corporate. "The most possible equalization of all the associates was laid down, as the fundamental constitutional principle. The undue rising and expanding of the more capable, was hindered in order that the less gifted should not be suppressed. Hence each industrial person or craftsman was compelled to join one of the guilds, and the number of apprentices and workmen, and in consequence the productive ability of the employer was regulated. Closely connected with this was the fixing of the rate of wages, the restriction of the number of masters of the craft, and the greatest security possible of a ready sale by excluding foreign productions." (Contzen). Besides this, the acquiring, as well as the artful practising of any profession was a matter of strict oversight and vigilance. Thus these fraternaties for centuries have operated upon and affected most beneficially the standard of the craft itself, as well as the economic, moral condition of the family, and the commonwealth, and the formation of the Social Question in general, although all of them more or less had the character of feudal coercion stamped upon them. In the course of time, however, these guilds, as at last all human creations do, became accessible to corrupting influences and abuses, and of necessity degenerated. For a time, and under the prevailing social abnormities, they served a good purpose; but were very far from solving the social problem, which from generation to generation assumed a most threatening attitude. The fundamental principle of enslaving the personality and liberty of man, underlying all feudal institutions and counter schemes, gradually worked itself out in such a manner, that at last the pressure became intolerable, and reason, emotions, and hands revolted.

Just before the dawn and during the time of the Reformation, the agricultural conditions especially, had become so crushing, that the peasants began the well-known "Peasant Wars." But their history, as well as that of other communistic commotions of that and the subsequent periods,—as of a Seb. Frank, Thomas Minster and others, is sufficient evidence, that the entire national economy, and the movements of culture at this time pressed forward toward a breaking loose from the past. Society had reached a crisis, which imperatively demanded a radical change of the political affairs, as well as of the social. As for economics, a new system gradually and unawares rose on the ruins of feudalism, which by degrees crumbled into the dust. In what way it was supplanted by the system of free competition, will be the object of the next lecture.

Before dismissing, however, this part of our investigation, it will be well to fix in our minds, the chief points of the historic development of the Social Queston as far as considered.

1). It admits of no doubt that the expressions of the Old and New Testaments on social and economic relations of human life were divinely intended, as rules and regulations for the conduct of those that profess to believe the Scriptures. Christianity especially, started out with the express purpose to permeate with its heavenly influence and power all earthly relations of human life. At its beginning it seemed to be most succeesful in this respect. But after a few centuries of its existence, it admitted and even fostered social conditions that were merely a slight alteration of the bondage of the Greek and Roman slaves. The Church, then, had lost its salutary influence. How are we to explain this strange appearance ? A careful study of the development of the doctrines and the practical life of the Christian Church, during the first four or five centuries convincingly reveals the fact, that the economical perversions of feudalism, are but the logical consequences of the spiritual decline of the Church. How could it be otherwise From the inner Godlike life of the Church, as from the fountain head were to go forth those mighty renewing influences, that were calculated to raise again all human affairs and conditions to the divinely fixed standard. But what, when the fountain became turbid ? Need we wonder at the unnatural, repulsive social conditions of society ? Certainly not.

2). The secularization of the Church resulted in the losing sight of the fact, that its ministry was that of serving, and not the cultivation of a domineering, lording spirit. Hence the gradual rise of popery with all its monstrosities. But this hierarchical principle naturally reflected itself in absolutism of state despotism on the one hand, and in the supreme arbitrariness of feudal prerogatives on the other hand. The one begat and upheld the other. The equality of all men before God was perverted into an undue distinction of a few, who in Church, state, and society, became the lords and masters, while the rest were

doomed to ecclesiastical, political, and economical servitude. This relation was even proclaimed, as a necessary
outgrowth of a natural law.

3). The degradation of the dependent classes began
with an unbecoming disregard of the personal moral worth
of man and with a depreciation of labor rendered, the
latter being but the logical consequence of the former.
These two distinctive features formed in fact the most
salient points in the Social Question from its very beginning.

And it is the consciousness of these oppressive evils,
that has caused the dependent classes to invent and devise
counteracting means, or in case of their failure, finally to
resort to acts of violence. A further investigation will
show this more clearly.

LECTURE II.

THE SOCIAL QUESTION UNDER THE REIGN OF FREE COMPETITION.

In the preceeding lecture we discovered the enslavement of the personal liberty of man, as the conspicuous signature stamped on the religious, civil, and social relations of the middle ages. The compulsory, coercive institutions of feudalism did not allow the self-existence of the individual to exert itself,—the laborer was, and remained unfree in spite of Church and religion. On the other hand they called forth contrary agencies, which on their part, though unconsciously, became instrumental in augmenting and aggravating, even this state of dependence. For in political, social, and economical life, everything was constituted and regulated in a corporative manner. The individual had no will of his own, but had to submit to the iron rules of the guild. Even the Church of that time executed the principle of corporative authority and constraint with the greatest severity, as the Roman hierarchy is doing still. The individual church-member in his belief, his personal convictions, yea, even in the dictates of his conscience was tied down to the authority, and the judgment of the church. Now, against this repression of the personality and of the personal rights of man, Protestant Reformation reacted, in asserting above all the personal title of the individual to all the means of grace in Christ Jesus, as well as his individual liberty, over and against ecclesiastical compulsion, and his own personal responsibility to the head of the Church. Self-evidently this Protestant position could not fail to exercise a powerful influence on the political, social, and economic relations of that time. The spirit of liberty which since the fourteenth century, in all these various conditions, had manifested its presence by various but disconnected signs, received new life form, and shape by the reformatory movement, and was led into the right track. The individual as such received again his due estimation.

But alas! It is too well known, that not long after the dawn of the Reformation this evangelical conception of liberty was transformed into that of abstract " *Individual-ism.*" That is, the individual was separated from the historical totality, and in matters of belief he was entirely placed on his own ability to think and to will. It was especially English deism of the seventeenth and eighteenth century, which, by its doctrine concerning religion, as a product of human nature, undermined the weight and authority of the revealed truth of God, thus placing the individual and his judgment over and above the decision of the Word of Light. *Humanity* and *nature* became the catch-words, and the ideal of the times.

In France these negative tendencies found all the more ready access, as the political, social, and economical monstrosities and contradictions of the country materially aided their introduction. Besides, since the days of *Hugo Grotius*, at the beginning of the seventeenth century, the so called *natural right* had developed itself, that is the idea, that on the part of nature, certain inalienable rights were granted to each individual, as to a human being. These pretended innate rights were placed over and against, yea, even above, the positive, Divine and the historically developed human right. In France it was especially *de Montesquieu*, who introduced and disseminated these ideas, especially in politics; while *Rousseau*, in his " Contrat social," (On principes du droit publique 1762), gave expression and shape to them.

In economics, of course, the effect of these negative religious, and liberal political tendencies soon became visible. The arising liberal spirit here likewise attempted to throw off the burdensome chains of feudalism, and to create a new order of things. The first lasting effort of this kind was made on the part of the so-called *physiocrats* in France, whose most prominent leaders were Quesnay, Condillac, Turgot, and Mirabeau. Their first opposition was directed against *mercantilism*, or against that doctrine, which proceeded from the idea, that the individual, as well as the national well-being of a country, consisted mainly in the possession of *money*, for which reason especially, trade and commerce were to be raised, protected, and regulated. The physiocrats, on the contrary, maintained and asserted, " That the economic welfare of the country rested on the clear gain of every private economy." For this reason they considered only that portion of the population, that engaged in agriculture, the cultivation of forests, land, and mining, as the proper productive elements of the people, while the merchants, manufacturers, the literati, yea, to some extent, even the artisans, appeared to them more or less, as unproductive drones. In this manner the followers of this new doctrine were trying to raise again that class, which had been trodden down mostly by feudalism, namely, the tillers of the ground.

In politics the opposition turned against the absolutism of the state, and the prerogatives of the feudal ranks and orders. Against these it was maintained, that also the economic production possessed a right, in as much as it rested on the "ordre naturel,"—a natural order, and, therefore could claim " a droit naturel," a natural right. Consequently, the state wrongfully exercised the right of interference, being warranted only to observe the policy of "laissez faire et aller." (That is, in as much as everything would develop itself best by itself, or by necessity of nature it would be best to let things have their own course).

Now, in expressing an opinion on physiocratism, it must be admitted, that a certain right of existence cannot be denied to it. Nay more, when compared with feudalism, we must recognize in this system a considerable progress. But nevertheless, it cannot be denied that serious errors cling to it, which in the course of time have exerted a detrimental influence. Its fundamental mistake is the attempt, to build itself up on the false basis of those so-called rights of nature and of a natural development. Misled by the speculative enlightening philosophy of the times, the physiocrats proceeded from something imaginary, and untenable, and paid no regard to the real wants and primary conditions of national economy. As a natural consequence, they laid the foundation to an economical division of society, which in the subsequent periods has worked disastrously. This has been especially the case since the senior master of classical economy, *Adam Smith*, in his book : " Wealth of Nations," has arranged the respective doctrines of the physiocrats into a scientific system.

In England at that time serfdom was actually, though not by law, abolished. Industry, commerce, and navigation, had been raised to an astonishing degree of prosperity. Labor, there in the economical, as well as the scientific movements of the people, stood in the foreground. Yet even here, the mercantilistic idea was prevalent, consequently political economy was made an object of the supervision of the state.

Adam Smith, on the other hand put forth efforts to free it in every respect from the civil guardianship, and to place it independently on its own foundation. In his personal intercourse with the physiocrats and encyclopedists of France, he had found ample opportunity to learn their tenets. In his own religious views he evidently stands on the ground of the empiric materialistic drift of his time. Hume, Rousseau, and Kant had essentially influenced the religious conceptions of Smith, as has been demonstrated by *Onken* in his book : "Smith und Kant."

Now, as for the system of this great economist, it is well to observe, that it is a well formed, scientific superstructure, reared and enlarged on the basilary principles of physiocratism. As its cornerstone may be considered the axiom: "Industry or human labor, is the source of all wealth." And it will be all the more productive and

renumerative, the more it will be able to produce goods
for exchange. Free, unchecked self interest is always to
be regarded as the only impellent force in economic life
and activity, and this for the following reasons:

First—Because self-interest, according to this system,
is an inherent law of nature; secondly, it alone is capable
of stiring up the capitalist to undertakings (enterprises);
thirdly, because, all activity springing from it, is better
calculated than external force or influence to advance the
economic welfare of the community, and to harmonize
the various interests.

For each economic person the following alleged indisputable laws of nature are claimed: First—The *absolute*
right in all relations of economic life and intercourse, to
be allowed to move about free and unobstructed, and to
be entitled to the same rights as others.   From the nature
of the case, of course, ungrown persons (children) and
women form the only exceptions. Secondly, the *natural
right*, to possess at will and in every possible way *private
property* or *capital*, as a means of production, and to dispose of the same in an absolute manner even to abuse;
thirdly, the full power to make contracts with others for
the purpose of securing self interest; and lastly, the prerogative by will and testament to dispose of the acquired
possessions, even beyond the limits of natural life.   In
the sphere of state polity, this system admits the right of

interference, but like the phys:ocrats it insists that all functions consequent thereto, are to be restricted to such exceptional cases, which private economy is unable to man-
age successfully, as for example, the maintaining and
administering of public justice, general education, and
the guaranty of military protection *ad extra.* This latter
position is especially defended by the so-called Manchester school, founded 1839 as the extremest faction of the
followers of this system.

Two most important political events gave a mighty impulse to this liberal economical movement, namely, the
outbreak of the French Revolution, and the Declaration
of Independence of the United States. The former with
its worldshaking success, added materially to the breaking
apart of the morbid feudal institutions, while the latter
opened a wide door to free trade, production, and consumption.

The new order of things was hailed by thousands, as
the dawn of a new and prosperous era. Actually it came to
pass what had been predicted of its rapid progress and
spread, namely that during the coming generations it would
rule the world. The classical economy, founded by
Smith and Ricardo, is swaying its sceptre in every civilized country of the globe. And what is more than that,
until very recently high and low have considered, "Its
dogmas, as Roesler, Die Grundlehren, etc., says, as the

irrefutable results of strictly scientific researches, its conceptions as admirable products of the nicest and deepest labor of thought, and its practical usefulness has appeared raised above every doubt. To question the doctrines and tenets of this theory was considered unnecessary and inadmissable, if not dishonest, a crime against sound human reason, nay, what is worse, as an attack on the thought of liberty of the present time."

And yet, a closer examination of Smithianism reveals many a weak point, that invites our criticism and calls forth our decided dissent.

Let us look, for example,

I. AT ITS INNER VALUE.

When we consider the circumstances under which the system of free competition sprung into existence, and keep in our minds the generating powers, giving life to it, then its origin is, certainly, not calculated to arouse our enthusiasm, especially when we, as we ought to, bring it to the test of the Word of Truth. For even this condensed historical review has convinced us, that in economics this industrial system exhibits but the deposit or sediment of the naturalistic, materialistic, and rationalistic tendency of the times. It was born out of that spirit, whose characteristic signature is an entire breaking loose from all Divine authority and every higher order. The so much applauded classical economy of Smith and his followers is evidently based on that well-known "Naturalism," which from that time on to our days has wielded such a pernicious influence. This is manifested from the fact that the entire system in all its laws, regulations, considerations, aims, and ends, is governed by the hypothesis of an absolute and abstract order of nature, ruling social and economic life, as well as the material world. Smithianism does not deduce the necessary laws for industrial movements from man, as the most vital, because self-conscious moral and accountable factor of production. Neither does it reflect that on account of the mental, spiritual, and religious nature of man, human life in all its manifestations is to be governed by higher, than mere natural and material laws. Man in this system is considered only from the standpoint of materialism, namely, as a natural force to be employed and recompensed in the process of production as every other power of nature. To prove this allow me, first, to call your attention to the position which *labor* occupies in the present industrial system. Its avowed "Naturalism" does not allow it to regard this primary factor of production, as a professional achievement of a human and moral being, but merely as a *technical* action, intended for a technical effect. Naturally, therefore, the laborers are not considered as a distinct class of society, forming a potent element in the cultural development of mankind—but only as an other class of technical means, which must come under the same laws, which regulate the production and exchange of goods. Hence labor appears in the market for sale under the same conditions, that rule the purchase of every other article of merchandise. And as a necessary and natural consequence, the workman is engaged and renumerated according to the law of demand and supply. In other words, merely external circumstances and mechanical relations decide the value of labor, fix the height of wages, and determine the weal and woe of the laborers. But placing ourselves on the foundation of Christian principles, can we for a moment doubt, that such purely material considerations are anything but materialistic?

Moreover, when labor is represented as the only source of private and public wealth, such a view is but the logical consequence of the naturalism pervading the whole liberal system. For if in the production of wealth general causes, over which the individual has no control, were recognized labor would loose its prestige and its claims. But it is a daily observation, that the so-called "Conjunctures" of trade and traffic, that is: "The totality of technical, economic, social, and judicial conditions of society," exercise a mighty influence on the formation of private or public gain or loss. Very often, and that par-

ticularly under the reign of free competition, weal and
woe of the individual are dependent on the co-operation
of these external agencies, so that he is by no means
always the manufacturer of his own luck or misfortune;
but many a time merely the victim of unfavorable economic combinations, and questionable transactions, or the
darling child of ever prosperous contingencies. Or in
more accurate and becoming language, All-ruling Providence, and by his permission, the conduct of man to man
is not to be left out of account, when the question as to
source of human welfare is raised. But this fact is overlooked, yea on purpose set aside by the system of the
physiocratic school. Hence no attention is paid to those
social and moral regards, and duties, which result from
the recognition of this all-important truth. Smithianism
is guided only by material or natural considerations.
How far the axiom, that labor is the only source of wealth
by a process of reasoning, has been instrumental in producing socialism, will appear in our next lecture.

The extreme materialistic character of the system of
free competition is especially evident from the position to
which it raises *self-interest*. It is true this natural impulse
is found in every human being, and even in Holy Scripture, it is recognized as an important element of human
activity and self-preservation. [1 Thess. iv : 11, et seq.;
1 Tim. v. 8] But when physiocratism elevates self-

interest to the import of a law of nature, and declares it to
be the exclusive motive power in economy and industry,
then it hands itself over completely to materialism. For
it is the most essential characteristic of materialism to
transform a mere necessity of nature into a binding coercive law for the social and economic life of man. So
in this case, self-interest furnishes an inducing reason,
or an impulse for the human will and its resolutions—we
all heed its promptings more or less, and are led by it in
our actions. But that does not imply, that in all these
cases self interest acts upon our decisions with the power
of an irresistible law of nature. On the contrary, when
we lift ourselves above the conceptions of the naturalistic
view of the world; when we place ourselves under the
enlightening influence of the spirit of Christianity, then we
become aware of the fact that self interest has degenerated
into selfishness, egotism, avariciousness, etc.; and that,
on that account it ought not in every case decide our
actions. In other words, the Christian conscience feels
constrained to subject its urgings to the ruling of the
Divine law of love to God and to man, as the highest aims
and ends of his life. Political economy, undoubtedly,
gravely violates the Divine precepts and principles of justice, equity, and philanthropy, when it assigns to self
interest the import of a dogma, and considers it the primary, as well as the final purpose of all social and econ-

omic movements. Its materialism is evident, and will appear still more so, when we examine its pretended *claims*.

As was stated at the beginning, the liberal economy, in full harmony with its basal naturalism, has not only asserted, but also obtained legal recognition of the following four laws: *The law of absolute liberty of the economic person. The absolute right to private property or productive capital. The right of free contract. And the absolute disposal of possessions by means of will and testament.* As the liberalistic literature of the former, as well as of the present century considers self-interest of the same necessity and import, as the laws of the material world, it does not hesitate to affirm that the economic acts of man, proceeding from the human will, are also subject to the natural laws. And as self-interest is the only motive power impelling man to actions, it must have absolute sway, must not be checked. The fallacy of such reasoning, is obvious, as we have seen already. If, indeed, the alleged laws or rights were natural in the sense claimed for them, then they would have been in operation at all times, and in every place, where economic subjects were found. But of such a universal existence and activity of natural social laws, history knows nothing. Smithianism commits a serious blunder by looking upon the entire economic development, as upon a natural organism, which out of itself took the present form, nay which could not but assume such a shape. It is true, the present economic orders and formations are not the product of arbitrariness,—they present a historic development. But the system of economy or industry is, nevertheless, also an artificial organization, which has been created and planned for a specific purpose through the agency of acts of the human will and by rational calculation, dexterity, and energy. For this reason it is folly to talk about economic rights, as natural laws, they are merely temporary rules and regulations, by which, for the time being, industry, trade, commerce, etc., are governed, and that by common consent or otherwise.

It is equally absurd and perverse to claim *absoluteness* for the exercise of these economic rights.

This idea proceeds from a disregard of the relation of man to his God, and to his fellowmen. It ignores the fact, that the social conditions of the individual are but the result of the only absolute will of his Maker, and the sovereign workings of his providence. It sets aside the obligation, springing out of man's utter dependence on his God, to use all his social privileges with a view to his accountability to the Supreme Ruler of the universe. The erroneous conception, of liberalism also fails in perceiving, and carrying out the right relation of man to man. Unfortunately, it has succeeded in establishing the present social laws, to make its utterly false conception of society the legal basis of those economic rules and orders. In the sense of the liberal economy, society is not an inner unity, but an external coexistence of human beings. Hence the individual is independent, autocratic, and autonomic. But the perverseness of such an idea is evident. The individual is not only dependent on the historically developed society, of which either by birth or otherwise, he forms a component part, but innumerable relations of life render him dependent on the community in general, as well as on the separate parts thereof. Any social or economic right, therefore, that he may enjoy, he possesses by and through the commonwealth, and that with the implied understanding, that he exercise his privileges not only for his own benefit, but also for the welfare of his fellowmen, and especially for the higher purposes of the body politic. The very idea of society is based on the principle of the Divine law of love to men. Hence the asserted absoluteness of private rights is a materialistic assumption.

Entering, however, into particulars and beginning with the alleged right of absolute liberty of the economic person, it will be noticed, that since the latter half of the last century this is considered as the only preliminary condition for the attainment of private and public property. Hence the right is claimed for each individual, to enter the econ-

omic race-course without being physically compelled
thereto, or restrained from it.   Liberty is demanded, to
produce at any time, and in any place, also the right without regard for the interests of others to turn their unfavorable physical, mental, and economic circumstances to
self-advantage.

Now, it cannot be denied that economic liberty is the
most essential means for the promotion of production.
Nevertheless, liberalistic legislation, has made a grave
mistake in legally sanctioning the principle of absolute
liberty in the form in which materialistic economy presented it.   For, as Roesler, truly says [p. 47]:   "The
law-giver has not only to consider the interest of production
and of the producers, but he has also, when he orders legislative measures for the advancement of production, to
inquire how far they will also serve a just and humane
distribution; what influence they will have on the formation of the personal condition of the workman, upon
family life and other moral conditions; and how they will
bear upon the realization of the moral objects of the
state."   But it is a sad fact that neither political economy
in formulating private rights, and legislation in issuing
the same, on the whole has not paid that attention and
consideration to these vital regards, which it ought to
have done.   It is for this reason, that the right in question for the greatest part has worked in and for the

interest of the economically strong, while to the weaker elements of society it has proved a disadvantage. But a law that gives full sway to egotism, that does not take into account the vast inequality of the economic subjects, and that merely aids the material pursuits of society, such a law cannot stand when tested by the Divine principles of justice and equity.

The same is true with reference to the second asserted claim of the liberal system: *The absolute right to private property or productive capital* (jus utendi et abutendi re sua). Liberalism defends this claim by pointing us to its absolute necessity for the economic process. It is said to be the only powerful incentive to saving, by means of which the wasted or worn-out means of production are always replaced, and the great and puzzling problem of furnishing the necessary means for the satisfaction of all possible economic wants of the people is solved. From these facts, then, is deduced the natural right of the individual not only to possess private property, but also to increase the same to any possible amount and freely to use it for the various purposes of production.

In replying to this reasoning, we do not for a moment hesitate to admit, that thus far no other economic factor has been able to reach better or even the same ends, that private property has done. Nay, more than that: Private property rests as to its right of existence in the will and

designation of God, as we have seen in our previous
lecture. But notwithstanding, yea just on account of
that admission, we maintain against this asserted right
the same objections that we have raised against the
naturalism and the principle of absolutism, underlying all
these pretended claims. For the very fact that property
is an ordinance of the Creator, lifts it above the will, the
arbitrariness, or pleasure of the individual, as well as of
society in general. Hence, the dispositions of possessions must be in harmony with the declared authoritative
purposes of God. But if anywhere in industry, it is in
the position assigned to private property, where political
economy has ignored Divine principles, and allowed the
unchristian conceptions of the Roman law to formulate
its legal social relations. For all the privileges demanded, as above stated, for the accumulation and application of productive capital, are not prompted by that
objective moral law, which has emanated from the being
of the Supreme Law-giver, but by the dictates of egotism.
But the Roman law on this point, as has been justly remarked, is but the legal expression of grandiose egotism.
Besides, the present ruling system of industry does not
make any moral demands on the acquisition of property,
nor on its disposition. All that is required of the economic person is the prevention of an open conflict with
the rights of another—exactly the position which

the Roman law observes. Judging, however, from the standpoint of the Word of Truth, we are compelled to declare this Roman, pagan conception, as standing in direct opposition to the biblical idea of the right to property. If our former exposition is correct; then the individual right in this respect emanates from the moral law of God. Consequently, it is in force whether the economic person is enabled to maintain it or not; or whether the state guarantees it to him or not. But in accordance with that higher law, every acquisition must be "well-acquired," must in every case be obtained by morally allowable means in order to become property, otherwise it is considered as theft. Besides, every righteous possession puts the owner thereof under solemn obligation, to use and apply the same to moral ends and purposes. Now measure the right in question by these Divine rules and requisites, and its materialistic character becomes obvious.

The right to *free contract* is supported, by calling our attention to the fact, that the individual could not employ his faculties and material means to his own, or the advantage of others, unless the privilege be granted to him to associate himself with others for the purpose of securing a more profitable and expeditious mode of production. By so doing the scattered physical, intellectual, and industrial forces, are combined to an harmonious action and achieve astonishing results. The capitalist is enabled by means of a division of labor, and by producing on a larger scale in a shorter time to repay himself, and to satify the economic wants of the community sooner and more effectively.

Now justice demands that we give all well deserved credit to the achievements accomplished by way of partnership, associations, and wholesale trade, and manufacture. There is, likewise, neither morally nor economically anything to be said against the principle underlying the right of contracting, for the purpose of gaining larger advantages. But at the same time, it must be maintained that the form in which this economic right is presented, and legally recognized entirely ignores the higher law of God, as well as the social law of common interest. Thus, for example, every contract as to the compensation of labor is considered legally valid, as long as the parties concerned by their own free will give their consent to the stipulations of the agreement. Neither may any of them claim a right or privilege, that cannot be deduced from the express terms of the bargain made. An appeal to a higher law is out of question. But there is just the point, where this pretended right fails to come up to the Divine standard. It utterly disregards the claims of common interest, and permits the individual to take every possible advantage of the un-

favorable physical, intellectual, and industrial conditions
of others. How far in this respect, it has caused enormous evils, will be considered presently.

The physiocratic idea of the *right of disposing by will*
is closely connected with its wrong view concerning property. If a person by a law of nature is permitted to use
his possessions at will, it very naturally follows that he
can dispose of the same even beyond the limits of his natural life. Besides, there is, undoubtedly, a great deal of
truth in the assertion, that persons are more apt to save
and to accumulate their savings, when they can rest
assured that they will be preserved intact to their heirs.
And who would gainsay the assertion, that each individual
saving adds also to the national wealth and lifts industry
to a higher standard. All this is very true; neither would
we question the correctness of the opinion of the great
jurist, *von Scheele*, when he says: "Property and the right of
making a will belonging thereto, are without doubt, the
necessary and natural foundations of human society.
They are so necessary and natural for social man as air
and light are for physical man. For, in order that a higher
culture can develop itself at all, the regulation and ordering of the priveleges of the members of a commonwealth
concerning the things by which they live, is indispensable.
Especially, the distribution of the economic goods among
the living, and the re-distribution of the same, in case of

death, must be done according to principles previously determined and valid in general."

But all this does not prove that the present institute and order of inheritance is the only perfect and just one. It is well known that the same is derived from the old *Roman* conception of right. But that concerns itself exclusively about the individual, and does not recognize any regard for society. Now this liberal doctrine just overlooks the important fact, that the industry and gain of the individual is not possible except in connection with the industry and trade of society. From this, as well as from the state, each industrial individual constantly receives assistance in acquiring wealth, though very often it may not be known to, or acknowledged by the economic subject. Consequently a part of the economic success is always due to the community even if it cannot be determined in so many round figures. The above named jurist, von Scheele, therefore, states the case correctly when he proceeds: "Now, whereas the body politic always steps in, in case of failure on the part of the economic individual, by means of provisions for the poor or other subsidiary institutions, while taxes in general are to be considered merely as a recompense for furnishing and granting the foundation for economic life and activity, which, indeed, would not be extant in its present form without the regulation on the part of the state, therefore the title of the commonwealth to a joint participation in the economic successes by way of hereditary right, cannot be doubted." Hence the assertion of the physiocratic school concerning this fourth pretended natural right needs correction. Of course, it is entirely within keeping of the tendency of the whole system, which like the Roman right recognizes nothing but the egotism of the individual, and unfortunately, "Right is the religion of egotism."

Utterly false is finally also the physiocratic Manchester idea concerning the *state*. According to it the duty of the same consists merely, in the production of *security* or *protection*. That is to say, to it is assigned the part of a night-watchman, whose duty it is to guard the safe of the rich, as Lassalle expresses it. It is true, the first object of the state is to create in the interior or home-department rules of laws for its subjects, and to maintain the same *ad extra*. But certainly, its functions are not exhausted thereby. Its aim and end is also culture and welfare in general; and this feature of its purpose results from its moral nature or character. In this respect the state is bound to provide those conditions and relations, by which the physical, economical, ethical, and religious interests of the individual, as well as of society can be promoted. But how is the state to fulfill this mission, unless directing, controlling, and restraining power, is given to it? Of course, egotism is somewhat checked, when such a prerogative is granted to the state; and, as the entire system is built on self-interest, we need not wonder at all, that one of the most important functions is denied to the civil organism. Physiocratism is nothing but individualism, while the fundamental idea of the state is the securing of the *common* interests of *all*, i. e., of society against any threatening particularism. Consequently social circumstances may not only permit, but even require the state, energetically to interfere with the economic management of the individual, as well as of national economy in general. And in fact this indisputable right is exercised in various ways by each government, and that not in accordance with, but in spite of the physiocratic doctrine. But whether this civic function receives its full attention, is a different question which, however, will be an object of later consideration.

Now, summing up the whole thus far, we are justified in saying, that the system of free competition rests on entirely false principles, axioms, and claims. And they, single and collective, are directed to one sole end: the establishment of individualism or egotism. The natural consequence is the atomizing of society and all its interests. Here then, we have just the opposite of what was intended by that wonderful economic legislation of the Old Testament, and by the introduction of the spirit of Christianity of the New. A reform, therefore, is highly necessary.

But here, we are met with an imposing array of brilliant successes, which free competition pretends to have achieved. In every possible tune, the advantages of this economic system over all the others preceeding it, are sung, and the avowers of the Manchester idea see nothing, but sheer gain and excellence in it. For this reason we are compelled, secondly, to examine a little more closely

ITS OUTER ADVANTAGES,

in order to be enabled to form a correct opinion as to its adaptation to social purposes.

And, here let me say at the outset, that it would be folly to deny the astounding progress that has been made in the sphere of economic activity and enterprise, since private capital has assumed the reign. For example, the technical improvement of the method of production, the essential diminution of the productive expenses, the enormous augmentation of industrial goods on the one hand, and the shortening of the time of labor on the other,—all these and other achievements are things which the feudal times did not in the least anticipate. Besides, the division of labor has developed to a marvelous degree human talent, art, and inventive faculty, and rendered known and unknown powers serviceable to industrial ends. In like manner facilities for traveling, locomotion, and international inter-communications, have been called into existence, that leave former times entirely in the shade. Socially and economically the physiocratic system has worked a complete revolution, and if the present indications do not entirely deceive, then industry has but reached the eve of still greater improvements and facilities. All this must be admitted.

But at the same time we hold, that all these beneficial and surprising results are not produced by the system with the necessity and force of natural laws, as the admirers of it would have us believe. Justice requires us to say with the great economist Wagner: "Free competition possesses but the tendency to such advancements, but that does not invest it with any positive merit."

On the other hand when we place opposite the industrial gains, the numerous evils and disadvantages, which are the logical consequences of this system, and which actually have been originated by it, then its boasted excellencies begin to appear rather in a doubtful, negative light. Only a few of them we will subject to a closer consideration.

Every system of political economy, that lays claim to superiority or preeminence, must be able to prove, that it not only promotes the interests of a few, or of a small minority of the economic subjects; but that it creates and divides the national income in such a manner, that the totality of the population is enabled justly to participate in the distribution of wealth. Each advancement made on the economic field of human activity must transform itself into a progress of the total welfare of the whole people, if it is to be considered as a step in the right direction

Now, the question arises whether the system of free competition has secured a comparatively equal distribution of the national gain, or even attempted it. Unfortunately, we are constrained to say no; nay more, to assert that it has done just the opposite. And could we reasonably expect any other result? Certainly not; for a system which is constructed on the foundation of erroneous principles, as we have mentioned them before, and whose aspirations are all centred in egotism, such a system under the control of the sinful disposition of human nature and supported by the present order of society, must of necessity create injustice, discord, and tyranny. The reasons for this are obvious. For first, under such a system it is but natural, that those elements of society that are more favorably situated will always come out victorious and thus make *free competition* illusive, from the very start. People are, it is well known, by nature very *unequal* as respects their physical, mental, moral, and economic condition and capability. Now it is true, some of these inequalities may be ameliorated, or even be removed entirely by means of training, culture or legal protection.

But daily experience and observation confirm the fact,
that the great mass of people have been compelled to enter
the economic arena under extremely disproportionate conditions and prospects.   The result could not be doubtful,
in most of the cases those stronger at the outset obtained
the prize, while the weaker remorselessly were pushed
aside.   On the one hand all-devouring monopolies have
been formed, and domineering capitalists arisen, while on
the other hand we notice a host of dependent wage-earners.
That is, society has been gradually split into differently
situated classes, which socially and economically are
getting more and more solidified.   And what makes it all
the worse, the defenders of the system coolly look upon this
fact as the natural result of the Darwinian law of combat;
nay, they even hold that it is an immense gain for the
development of industry in general.   Thus purely human
volitions and actions are perverted into necessities of
nature, and the eyes and the hearts are shut against the
material, social and moral injuries inflicted upon society
by such glaring disruptions.

But there are also, secondly, *unscrupulous* elements
that enter the economic combat.   They, of course, will
watch every opportunity to further their egotistic, selfish
ends, even at the expense of the ruin of others.   To this
class, any and all means or measures are allowable, "The
use of which does not bring them openly into conflict with

the statute book." Now, it will be seen very readily, that the entire structure of the system of free competition is calculated to aid and countenance such nefarious elements, especially by the right of free contract. How far it has done so will be apparent when we look at the moral standard by which in general business transactions are measured in our day. It is an open confession, made by hundreds of conscientious business men, that at present it is well nigh impossible to conduct business transactions on strictly honest principles, if one is determined to hold his own in the commercial world. And never-ceasing complaints about, and discoveries of adulterations of articles of merchandise, misrepresentations, impairing of weights and measures, villainous exchange manoeuverings, stock-waterings, sham auctions and sales, and a host of other disreputable transactions more than confirm such confessions.

The system of free competition lays great stress on manufacturing and trading on a *large scale*. The more of the productive capital there is accumulated in the hands of one or more capitalists and circulated, or set in motion by them, the greater the net gain will be. For in this case, a division of labor and employment of machinery can be applied to much greater advantage than in a small business. Besides, by far a greater number of laborers can be concentrated for an industrial undertaking, and an agreement made with them by means of the system of wages. In this way, and by constantly increasing the working capital, the expense in production is reduced to a minimum, while the sources of income are multiplied. Hence wholesale industry has undoubtedly achieved very favorable technical and economic results. But at the same time this kind of production exhibits so many injurious effects, that its advantages are more than counterbalanced. A few may here be mentioned.

It is a matter of constant observations, that the means of production are concentrating more and more in the hands of a few. Capital is clearly showing this tendency. The natural consequence is that smaller enterprisers are pushed aside, and the number of independent capitalists is continually diminished, while on the other hand that of depending wage-workers is rapidly increasing. Former masters and well-to-do producers by means of this business mania, have been driven into the ranks of impotent workingmen. Thus the entire social structure of society has changed. On the economic ladder there is room only on a few higher, or on numerous lower rounds, —those on which the middle class was accustomed to stand are breaking out more and more. And the lower strata of society either intuitively or by agitation have been awakened to a keen perception of this unnatural and oppressive state of affairs. They find themselves to a

great extent shut out from the higher means of culture
and education, and in many an instance even deprived of
the necessary means of support. In other words a *proletariate* has been formed, that is, a social class of such
as in the industrial turmoil have been thrown aside,
and which now are becoming more and more conscious
of that fact. As a natural consequence we observe dis-
satisfaction, discord, contention, clashing and a social
tension in general, that of late has assumed a threatening attitude.

Moreover, these social disruptions are nourished and
brought to a sharper point yet, by the conviction forcing
itself upon the minds of the laboring class, that the distribution of the constantly increasing national income, is
made to their still greater disadvantage. The workingmen of to-day are fully aware of the fact that capitalism has learned systematically, under the cover of the
right of free competition, to make it impossible for them
to share in a just manner the net gains. Thus, for
instance, the marvelous technical improvements in the
method of production, the introduction of machinery,
have not only set aside thousands of laborers, but enabled cold-blooded capitalism, to employ at a reduction
of wages *women* and *children*. By so doing the prospect
of men for work has changed for the worse, the value of
labor is depreciated and the rate of wages brought down

to the lowest point.   English and continental wage and labor-statistics fully confirm this assertion.

Now, " If the petty earnings of women and children, even finally would add to the income of the laboring family, some comfort might be drawn from these sad figures.   But under the present circumstances, when the supply is always larger than the demand, a lasting increase cannot be thought of.   The head of the family, who for weeks goes from door to door to find work, and who is always in danger of being thrust aside entirely, is satisfied at last with any amount of wages, that together with the earnings of his family will be sufficient for the prolongation of their distressed lives." (Schippel.)

This sad condition is aggravated by the right of *free contract* and of *unrestrained migration*.   The former enables capitalists to draw anywhere on surplus workingmen, while the latter gives them the power to fix their own conditions in the labor market, and to engage the necessary hands at such rates as the law of supply and demand will permit.   Under such circumstances the applauded right of free contract, as far as it concerns the laborer, is simply a farce.   For, if statistics are to be trusted, then on an average one-fifth of the working forces is at present and has for years been doomed to idleness. (Schippel, Mod. Elend, p. 56.)   Thus to the workman is, indeed, left the liberty of his arms and legs; but as to the rest, he is placed before the alternative, either to work at the rate proposed to him, or to go without work.

These grave charges the liberal system has been trying to repel by calling our attention to the acknowledged amelioration of the conditions of the laboring class, when compared with that of former times, and to the increased number of deposits in the savings-banks. The surplus of unemployed forces in the market is attributed to the unavoidable operation of the *law of population*, and to *overproduction*. Let us test these objections by existing facts.

Admitted even that the standard of wages, as well as of frugality, presents a more favorable aspect now, as compared with that of the laboring class of former times, the question still remains, whether on an average, the share of the workman in the net gains has been enlarged just in the same ratio, as private capital and the national income have increased. The objection will not hold good as long as this question cannot be answered in the affirmative. But when we consult the accessible statistics of all civilized countries, we receive a decidedly negative answer. For example the minute statistical labors of *Baxter*, *Porter*, *Baines* and others in England, touching this very subject, furnish indisputable proof " That the income of the laboring classes in spite of the enhanced productivity of labor has dwindled down to a constantly diminishing fraction of the entire national income; while on the other hand the income of the *possessing* classes exhibits a constantly swelling portion of the public profit. This result is not in the least affected by the larger number of deposits. For, according to the miscellaneous statistics, an English Blue-book, a few years ago 765,232 persons had deposited into the different savings-banks of England £20,991,075; of that sum only £1,365,700 were owned by 560,172 depositors, while the remaining 205,060 depositors represented a sum of £19,625,375. That is, 74 per cent. of the depositors had a claim to only 6 1-2 per cent. of all the deposits, while on the other hand, 26 per cent. were in the possession of nearly 93 per cent. of the entire capital. But who were those 560,172 depositors? Not capitalists, but working-men; for none of their deposits exceeded £10. Now, if capitalism could furnish proof that this disproportion in the number and the amounts of deposits in savings-banks had constantly changed in favor of the working class, then it would be justified in drawing from that fact a conclusion, as to the general improvement of the conditions of the workingmen. But statistics do not show such a favorable turn. On the contrary, the opposite will be shown in another connection.

As regards *overpopulation*, the political economists of this school are accustomed to charge that to the account of the *law of population*, as formulated by *Malthus*. According to it any given population has the tendency if no special disturbances occur, to double itself in the time of twenty-five years ; that is, it will advance from period to period in *geometrical progression* (1, 2, 4, 8, 16, etc.), while on the other hand, the means of subsistence at best can be multiplied by production only in *arithmetical progression*, (1, 2, 4, 6, 8, 10 etc.). The result of the relation of these two laws of nature to each other, is the fact that every population will soon reach the limit of the means of subsistence necessary for its maintenance; and when that boundary is overstepped, then poverty and misery are the unavoidable consequences. In other words, according to Malthus nature at the end does not provide sufficiently for the children she begets. Now, the liberal system under consideration has applied these reasonings of Malthus to the movements of political economy, and thereby discovered the alleged calming fact, that the overcrowded labor-market, and the need, and misery of the working classes are but the natural workings of these laws. But such conclusions are by no means warranted.

For, to speak in the words of Oettingen: "In no state of the civilized world, this sentence touching the movements of population can be substantiated by facts; because on the one side, as Malthus himself admits, an unchecked increase of the population takes place nowhere, and on the other hand, if chemical analyses of late prove anything, then the productive power of the soil is, indeed, not inexhaustive but unquestionably great, and at all events practically incalculable, when such uncultivated or meagrely tilled tracts of land are considered, whose productiveness can be increased yet a thousandfold.'' Nay, more, social and economic statistics of that so highly civilized country, England, furnish us with the following facts: Industry, as well as the production of raw material, and farming clearly show a constant advance in the net gains of labor. This increase was actually enormous during the last thirty years, as will be seen from the national income of *England* when estimated in money. According to *Young* this amounted for England and Wales in the year 1770, to £122,000,000, while at present it represents the stately sum of £1,200,000,000. We notice, therefore, a tenfold increase since the year mentioned. Now what has been the advance of the population during the same period? The statistics answer: England's population to-day is but three times as large as that of 1770. Compared with the progress of the population the national income, therefore, has tripled itself— indeed a convincing demonstration of the fallacy of the Malthusian theory.

Besides, these surprising results have been obtained in

spite of the fact, that on an average almost one-fifth of the workingmen, and the means of production have been laying idle. Hence the productiveness of the country was always greater than the actual production, and still the latter shows a regular advance.

Now look at the other side. The assessment registers of England show a steady advance of taxable property in the hands of the possessing classes. In many a case there is a five-fold enlargement. But the conditions of the working people do not exhibit any such improvement. The increase has always taken place in the higher regions of society. According to the statement of Schippel (p. 63), the laboring classes of England form 80 per cent. of the population, but they draw but 40 per cent. of the national income. The *highest* rank of society, however, represent not even 2 per cent. of the population and yet they command almost the same amount of capital, namely 36 per cent. That is, 235,600 persons divide among themselves an income of £297,200,000, while 10,961,000 must be satisfied with £324,600,000. Most assuredly over population, ever recurring dull business seasons, and massive poverty do not spring from an utterly false law of nature, but rather find their explanation in the incontrovertable fact, that the consumption of the economic goods is unable to keep step with the productivity of labor. In other words, massive poverty causes overpopulation; for "When the destitution of the masses and in consequence thereof the demand of goods remains stationary, then of course one portion of the laborers must become superfluous, as often as any progress in technics is made or the power of productiveness increased. But the totality of the laborers could be employed, when with an enlarged production of goods, their consumption among the lower classes would rise." (Schippel.)

Finally, we are obliged to raise this objection against the present system of free competition, that instead of causing a harmony of interests, it has brought about the greatest discord. This result, although perhaps not intended, is nevertheless not surprising, because it has reversed the maxim of fellowship: "One for all, and all for one," into that of individualism: "Each for himself and none for the other." The logical consequence shows itself in an unhealthy contention of interests between the different sources of wealth, between industry, trade, commerce, and farming, as well as between the enterprises of one and the same branch of economy. Thus very often the efforts and pursuits of members of one family, of one and the same part of the community, and of the different nations are at variance or come into contact with each other. How often have even bitter strifes and bloody wars been the final result of such combating interests!

Reviewing the whole we are driven to the conclusion, that free competition is an economic system, which in spite of its advantage over feudalism, as to its inmost nature is objectionable, and needs a thorough reform. Its injurious results socially, economically, and morally considered, demand speedy remedial counteractions; and this the more, as the working classes of our day cannot be hushed or appeased any longer by calling their attention to the glorious achievements of an unexcelled system. With them, the Social Question has reduced itself, to the practical query: how much do we get of the net gain of production? Unless free competition answers this question more satisfactorily than it has done hitherto, it does not require the gift of prophecy to predict the future. But, forsooth, Socialism may have come in as the rescuing angel, to deliver society from a final wreck.

LECTURE III.

SOCIALISM AS TO ITS DEVELOPMENT, ITS TENETS AND PURPOSES.

In our last lecture we merely touched upon the fact, that at an early date, opposition arose against the system of free competition, referring to the strictures that were made on its principles. We did, however, not say anything about a peculiar reaction that was caused by that system, and which at present is exerting itself with unusual power and fierceness. But our brief survey of the history of the social question would be very incomplete, if we should not say anything about the socialistic movement running in direct opposition to free competition. Besides, that time is gone by when Socialism is simply to be ignored. The sooner society will trouble itself about it, the less it may be troubled by it. But first of all it will be necessary to obtain a correct idea as to the character and design of this economic movement. Allow me, therefore, at this time to lay before you a succinct statement as to its development, its tenets and purposes; the next lecture being reserved to its criticism.

Socialism properly speaking, is the opposite of Individualism. In economics it presents that principle of order, which makes the interests of society and economy as of two totalities, the starting as well as the terminal point of its exertions; while Individualism pushes the interests and desires of the single economic subject into the foreground. Now, it has been justly said, that both of these principles are equally entitled to existence and regard. Neither can exclude the other entirely without seriously damaging the interests of society and economy. The just and proportionate blending together of the two, forms the proper solution of the social question. But efforts made to that effect are in our days not designated by the name of Socialism. We rather mean by it those exertions which aim at the entire extinction of Individualism in order to make the social principle the exclusive order of society and economy. Socialism in its modern sense is the complete negation of individualism. This much for the meaning of the term; now let us look at its origin and development.

It is generally assumed and asserted that Socialism in its present form, was the product of a few German cranks and knaves. What truth is there in this statement?

As early as the year 1793 a certain *William Godwin* published a book in London, entitled: "An inquiry concerning political justice and its influence on general virtue and happiness." 2 vols. In this work the author distinguishes "three degrees of property," or as we wouid term it, three forms of distribution of wealth or economic goods. "The first and simplest degree of property," Godwin continues, "is that, of my permanent right in those things, the use of which being attributed to me, a greater sum of benefit or pleasure will result, than could have arisen from their being otherwise appropriated." This principle, therefore, demands a division of property according to the needs and wants of the individual; a result, however, which Godwin does not expect unless a complete reformation of the spiritual and moral condition of mankind would take place.

"The second degree of property is the empire in which every man is entitled to the produce of his own industry, even that part of it, the use of which ought not to be appropriated to himself." This principle stands in opposition to the first and does not appear to Godwin as natural.

"The third degree is a system, in whatever manner established, by which one man enters into the faculty of disposing of the produce of another man's industry." (S. Menger, p. 42 ff). Property inherited, Godwin calls,

" misnamed wealth, or merely a power vested in certain individuals, by the institutions of society, to compel others to labor for their benefit." As to the relation of wages to income, for which no labor is rendered, Godwin cherished very unfavorable views. In order to remove these injurious conditions, he offers as a remedy " the dissolution of governments, the division of the historical, traditional state into independent sections, and the abolishing of legislative and executive state power. Only in extreme cases a national assembly is to be convoked. Individual economy as well as private property is to be continued, but each possessor thereof must be willing to resign his property for the benefit of others when necessity requires it.

Now, please notice the fact, that Godwin is entirely dissatisfied with the ruling economic system of his time, especially with the right in property obtained by the power of capital in " compelling others to labor for its benefit." That is to say, Godwin raises the very point which forms the fulcrum for the socialistic lever, applied to lift the present order of things off its hinges. His anarchistic views very fortunately remained without any effect on his time, but his socialistic theory exerted a noticeable influence; for in the year 1805 *Charles Hall* published a work: " The effects of civilization on the people in European states." In this and other writings Hall comes to the conclusion: " That in consequence of the steady increase of wealth, productive labor of the poor was constantly multiplied, while on the other hand, the income of the rich from idleness was getting enormous." In England, so Hall asserts, four-fifths of the population did not receive more than one-eighth of the product of their labor, the rest falling into the hands of the employers, in the shape of ground-rent or profit of capital. In order to do away with such unjust conditions, Hall insists " that everybody ought to work as much as was necessary for the maintainance of his family, and, that every one ought *to receive the full profit of his work.*" To accomplish this the English laws of primogeniture are to be abolished and " the refined industries" must be taxed heavily, so that the work of the poor will be restricted merely to the production of the necessaries of life. And as these two requirements are not sufficient yet for the end desired, the state has to expropriate the entire ground and soil, and to allot it permanently to the different families. But as these do not enlarge at the same rate, a re-division of the land will become necessary from time to time.

The peculiar feature of this proposed system is the combination of *collective* or State property, with private or individual economy, for which combination Hall referred to the agrar system of the Spartans, the Jews, and the Jesuites in Paraguay as precedents. In this respect he advances a step nearer to the socialistic idea of these days, which demands collective property with collective management thereof. (Menger, p. 45 ff.).

A more specifically socialistic and matured system we discover in the views of *William Thompson*, a scholar of Bentham, and of Irish descent. In his work published 1827: "An inquiry into the principles of the distribution of wealth most conducive to human happiness," he asserts the following as natural laws of distribution: " 1. All labor ought to be free and voluntary as to its directions and continuance; 2. All the products of labor ought to be secured to the producers of them; 3. All exchanges of these products ought to be free and voluntary."

Now, let me call your attention, just here, to the fact that Thompson starts from the same point from which the system of free competition proceeds: from the right of personal liberty of action; and yet he reaches an entirely different conclusion, namely, the right of the laborer to the full products of his exertions. Thompson also, like Smith and his followers, considers labor as the only cause of exchange-value, but from this supposed fact he deduces the juridical consequence, that the producer of value is also entitled to the full benefit thereof. " Secure," he says, "to the producer the free use of whatever his labor has produced." It is true, Thompson acknowledges that under the present order of things, the capitalist, to a certain extent, has a right to share in the products of labor in order to be repaid for the use of his buildings, machines, etc., but he does not want this restriction of the right to the full profit of labor to be made any further than absolutely necessary; and as for the actual carrying out of such a just principle of distribution, Thompson is very far from believing that under the present order of society it is, or can be done, expressing himself thus on that point: "The productive laborers stript of all capital, of tools, houses and materials to make their labor productive, toil from want, from the necessity of existence, their remuneration being kept at the lowest, compatible with the existence of industrious habits. The measure of the capitalists, on the contrary, would be the additional value produced by the same quantity of labor in consequence of the use of machinery or other capital, the whole of such surplus value to be enjoyed by the capitalist for his superior intelligence and skill in accumulating and advancing to the laborers his capital or the use of it."

Now, allow me to fix upon your minds the following three points: 1. Thompson considers it as a principle *of right*, that the producer of value should receive the full benefit thereof, with the exception admitted; but, 2. he *does not* get it; he is, on the contrary, kept at the lowest,

·compatible with the existence of industrious habits; and,
3. he *cannot* get it, because under the present order of
society capital claims the entire " additional or surplus
value," produced by labor. Keeping in mind these three
points you will directly discover in the writings of
Rodbertus, Marx and Lasalle, exactly the same range of
thought, the same reasoning and the very same language;
to me a convincing proof of the great influence exerted
by Thompson upon all the succeeding Socialists.

As to his remedial propositions, Thompson suggests,
above all, the establishment of communities, being influenced by the views of Robert Owen. But rather in
·opposition to his primary principle, the distribution of the
economic goods in these communities is to be made
according to the individual wants, while each healthy
member of society ought to furnish the same amount of
work, the time employed being the measure of exertion.
(Menger, p. 55-57).

In this connection various other writings, as for example those of John Gray, T. R. Edmonds, J. F. Gray,
etc., could be mentioned, but those adduced, undoubtedly
are sufficient to show that the germs of the present social
system, when considered in its scientific aspect, must be
looked for in English soil. This will become still more
apparent when the fundamental principle of Socialism;
the right of the laborer to the full product of his labor,

is kept in view. For, while the French Socialists of the eighteenth century, as *Morelly*, *Mably* and *Baboeuf* severely criticise the right to private property, as being the source of vice and egotism, none of them considers it as the means by which capital is enabled to prevent labor from enjoying the asserted right to its full benefit. Even *Saint Simon* (born 1760, died 19th of May, 1825) who has been styled the founder of Socialism, did not know the right to the full product; for he counts among the pre-eminently useful members of civil society, the most distinguished enterprisers and employers in the sphere of industry, trade and finance; the very classes which modern Socialism accuses of drawing their wealth out of the products of the labor of others. Of a somewhat more lasting effect proved *Fourierism ;* or the Ecole Societaire founded by *Charles Fourier* (born 1772, died 1837), and spread especially by Victor Considerant. The same proceeds on the observation of great poverty, which cannot be removed by the prevailing system of private economy. Hence property in land and capital is to be expropriated and common management to be introduced.

But strange to say, Fourier as well as his followers, were very far from adopting the principle that labor was entitled to its full product; on the contrary, they considered a great inequality of possessions in their proposed order of Society as unavoidable, as capital was to receive four-twelfths, labor five-twelfths and talent three-twelfths of the entire income.

In the meantime, however, the school of *Saint Simon* had taken a decided step towards the formation of modern Socialism. *Enfantin*, as well as *Bazard*, called attention to the contrast between those that lived of their labor, and those that were enjoying the products of the labor of others (travailleurs et oisifs). To them land rent and profit of capital, appeared as a tax levied on the workingmen by capitalists and owners of the soil, for the privilege of using their means of productions. Against this slavery of capital (l'esclavage des capitaux) the St. Simonists on the 9th of February, 1831, published their programme from which we take the following few sentences : " We demand the abolition of all hereditary privileges, without an exception; we demand the emancipation of the laborers and the forfeiture of the right of idleness, which consumes and blasts them. . . . We demand that the fruits of labor of the working classes, be not devoured by the idle classes, which are doing nothing nor save anything; who but love themselves. We desire a social order completely based on the principle: To each according to his capacity, to each capacity according to its works. We demand clearly the gradual suppression of all tributes which labor pays to idleness, under the divers names of farm-rent, recompense

for manufacture and capital" (Menger, p.67). As remedial measures the followers of this system suggest, among
others, a universal association of the people, a theocratic
organization of the state, and a transfer of the hereditary
right of the individual to the community.

A somewhat peculiar position is occupied by *Proudhon*,
who places himself on the fundamental principles of the
later St. Simonists, by pleading for the right of the laborer
to share in the net profit even after he had received his
wages. He is also an avowed enemy of private property
in its present form. But at the same time he bitterly
opposes the utopistic measures of socialistic communism,
and desires individual economy and free competition to be
preserved. In order, however, to reconcile these seem-
ingly conflicting ideas he proposes the creation of an exchange or people's bank (Banque d'exchange, banque du
peuple), which should make it possible to give a gratuitous
credit (gratuite du credit). By means of this, he expected land-rent and capital-profit to disappear. *Proudhon*,
however, never saw that bank, as the necessary capital
could not be raised. Fighting against Utopias he became
the victim of another, as he was trying to break the powerful influence of capitalism, guaranteed to it by right and
usage, by an impracticable arrangement.

Louis Blanc, another French Socialist, maintained that
all revenues from any other source than labor, were un-

just in themselves, but in the present order of right they had to be considered as absolute necessities. The economic equality. so much talked of in his time among all Socialists, consists with him only in " that proportionality which will exist in a veritable manner only then, when each one, after the law written by God himself upon his organization, will produce according to the measure of his faculties, and consume according to his wants." (Menger, p. 114 n. 4). In order to accomplish this and to counteract the evil influences of free competition, L. Blanc demands that the state, as such, supervise production. In each branch of industry the state has to erect factories, shops, etc , and thus to call forth a competition with the individual undertakings, which in this way he ex- pected to be compelled to fall in with the industries of the commonwealth. The state having thus obtained the upper hand, combines the similar manufacturies and workshops into associations, in order to prevent any con- flict of private interests. This mechanism is to be en- larged until a harmonious working together of all kinds of industry, trade and commerce will be established. Louis Blanc, therefore, did not intend to introduce a new economic principle, his object was, rather, to give a new direction to the existing social and economic factors. But in as much as he instigated the laboring and poor classes to active advances, in order to obtain the political

ascendency, he may be regarded as the founder of the
social democracy.   The working people expected from
the introduction of his system the salvation from all misery, but found themselves sorely disappointed and
deceived, when after a few months of trial, the established
national workshops proved a complete failure.   Besides
the revolution of the year 1848 for the present suppressed
all socialistic movements, as it brought *Cæsarism* on the
throne.

THE SO-CALLED SCIENTIFIC SOCIALISM.

Now, looking back for a moment, you will have observed that thus far all the socialistic efforts were moving
more or less on a Utopistic ground.   But during the 4th
decennium of this century, a *German* school of Socialists sprang into existence, which endeavored to give to
Socialism a philosophical basis, especially to prove its
principles of rights by philosophical deductions.   The
most prominent of that school is the well known trio,
Rodbertus, Marx, and Lasalle, none of whom however
can claim any originality as they are all dependent for
their thoughts on the sentiments expressed by the foregoing English and French Socialists.

Rodbertus sees in the different stages, through which
economic development thus far has passed, merely *historical* events, but not natural formations.   Consequently he
looks upon the individualistic method of production as

well as on private property and capital as upon historical categories, which may be altered and supplanted by others. He begins his dissecting criticism at the point of the *theory of value*, as advanced by Smith, Ricardo, and others of that school. Rodbertus accepts the theory, but he pushes it to its extreme conclusions. Says he in his second Social letter: " I connect with labor of society a productivity, which in all branches of industry, and particularly also in all branches of farming has increased very highly, and whose further growth is unlimited. But the 'natural' laws, which in industry and trade, left to themselves, and allowing property in land and capital, govern the distribution of the social product, prevent society from deriving any benefit from this advancement of productivity; for, on the one hand these laws are the cause that this distribution assumes the form of an ex-change-trade, under the rule of which the private owners of society-property in land and capital, are not permitted to allow production at all, or none to a larger extent than the opposite, corresponding ability to buy, is able to man-age. On the other hand these laws again are the reason why not only the product is divided between the latter (the capitalists) and the working classes, but why also the share of the workmen in the product is constantly diminished and consequently the ability to buy, of the majority of society is always reduced. This latter effect these laws bring about, by reason of the fact that labor, this creatrix of all productions, has also become an article of merchandise, which is paid, that is, receives its portion of the product according to the regulations of demand and supply. These laws under the present development of society turn out into a progressive measure to the disadvantage of those that possess this article; that is, the laboring classes, just while the productivity is enhanced. Thus these natural laws of industry and trade have become the cause why the increase of wealth, which from its very nature is designed only as a means of furthering the welfare and happiness of society, is turned into an occasion for its disturbance. Thus society is held by a magic circle, and placed in fatal contradiction to itself. Out of this deleterious circle, in which merely prejudices move it, society has to come out by substituting for the natural laws, as far as they are injurious, reasonable regulations."

This reasoning leads Rodbertus to the conclusion that private property and capital is to be abolished. But as he is averse to all political, especially to every revolutionary agitation, and as in his opinion the prejudices of the possessing classes cannot be removed at once, he expects, for this reason, an energetic interference from the state. He considers it its duty to regulate the question of wages, and gradually but peacefully to transmute the present state of things into that political order which shall be founded on merit or pure income-property. During this transition he is willing to allow to possession its full rent or revenue, if in the meantime the workingmen are permitted proportionately to participate in the general welfare. The plan of Rodbertus, undoubtedly, was profoundly conceived, and had not the least tinge of the present revolutionary socialistic movement. There is nothing of the hallucinations of an Owen or Fourier about it, who attempted a communistic commonwealth on a small scale. Rodbertus also had no sympathy with those of his time who advocated a division of the national wealth; his plan being, not the splitting up, but the unification of all private property and capital under the efficient direction and management of the monarchical state. After the decisive year 1870 in the history of Germany, he expected from Bismarck and the German empire an energetic attention to the social problem in the way proposed by him. Disappointed in this, he put himself in communication with the leading conservative socialists, without however, identifying himself with any social democratic measures.

Of a decidedly different character is his contemporary, *Carl Marx* (born 1818 at Trier), who, without doubt, took up the socialistic ideas of Godwin, Hall and Thompson, who, in the manner of Hegels dialectics, endeavored to digest and work them out critically and carry them into effect. Especially in his great work on "Capital" (1867) he proves himself a philosophic thinker and a reckless critic, who regards it as his task to tear down to the very ground, the existing social and economic structure. His political career and final exile undoubtedly, exercised a moulting influence on his mode of thinking and literary diction.   His sojourn in England afforded him a splendid opportunity of becoming acquainted with the economic conditions of the laboring classes, and to gather voluminous statistical material as to the social status of that country.

Marx, first of all, subjects to an unsparing criticism, capital, especially capitalistic accumulation that is, the present formation of movable, speculative means and sources of industry and income. According to his opinion, capital does not in the least add any value to the product, but labor does; as Smith and Ricardo had asserted before him; but, under the existing mode of production, labor always receives, in wages, but a fraction of its value, the remaining part flows into the pocket of the capitalist: he, therefore, enriches himself by other peoples property, which in this sense appears as "theft," as Proudhon had declared it. This private accumulation of capital Marx designates as "cheating, taking in, plus-making or draining others." Aside from this pressure, thus exerted on wages, this increase of capital is facilitated also by the extension of the time for labor, by technical acceleration of production, and by procuring cheap laboring men from other industrial centers. But, inasmuch as in the opinion of Marx under the present reign of the system of private economy or free competition, the individual is compelled to appropriate to himself this plus value or "theft," therefore, *private capital* and private industry is to be abolished and transformed into its opposite, into *collective* property, with public organization of labor. "Then the time of labor would be at the same time the measure for the individual share of the producer in the labor of the community, and would serve as a standard for the portion in the general product, consumable by the individual." (Schaeffle).

This radical change of the existing circumstances, Marx did not endeavor to bring about by the initiation of social reforms, as Rodbertus contemplated, but expected it only by means of a proletarian revolution. Without reserve he gives this as his opinion as far back as 1848, in a "manifest," which he issued in the name of and for the "Communistic League Society," organized in Cologne and London, when he writes: "The Communists assist (foster) every revolutionary movement intended against the existing social and political conditions. They openly declare that their purposes can only be reached by a forcible overthrow of all present orders of society.

May the ruling classes tremble before a communistic revolution. The Proletarians have nothing to lose except their chains, they have a world to gain by it. Proletarians of all countries, unite!"

Marx never swerved from these revolutionary sentiments; hence he regarded the organization of the " Internationale" in the year 1864, more as an instrument for agitation and for kindling class hatred, than as a means of organizing the interests of the working classes.

Now, when we compare Marx with Rodbertus, we at once discover a great similarity between their historical conception and judgment of the present abnormal economic conditions, so much so, that the question has been raised, whether Marx had not been influenced somewhat by the publications of Rodbertus. Be this as it may, it certainly admits of no doubt, that aside from these corresponding views Rodbertus in every other respect was just the opposite of Marx; for the former was of a thorough national bent of mind, while the latter had entirely lost his patriotism. Rodbertus exerted himself to remove the existing misery by calling upon the state to initiate the necessary reforms, hence his appeal to Bismarck. Even by his temporary connection with social democratic leaders he intended merely to exert a pressure from below on those on high. But Marx never believed in any reforms, but only in a complete clearing away of all economic and political forms and regulations hitherto in force; and to this radical idea he clung with such a mania, that he never put the question to himself, in what manner social conditions could and should be reconstructed again, after a successful revolution should have demolished everything.

As a theorist, Marx has rendered immense services to the socialistic movement. A certain *Fr. Engels* assisted him to a great extent, especially by the publication of his stirring work on " Die Arbeiterverhaltnisse Englands.'" (The Conditions of the Laboring Classes in England). He furnished, so to speak, the practical illustrations to the scientific deductions and sophisms of Marx.

But however great the influence of these three last mentioned thinkers may have been on the promotion of Socialism as a science, their effect on the laboring masses cannot be compared with that of a fourth and last one to be mentioned, namely with that of *Lasalle*. Being eminently gifted, possessing a thorough philosophical training, the adroitness and readiness of a jurist, and an overwhelming power of speech, he has rendered marked assistance to scientific as well as practical Socialism, especially among workingmen. It is true, he advances hardly any idea that had not been stated by French and the last named German socialists. He openly declares his great indebtedness to Rodbertus; but what hitherto had

been imprisoned between the covers of scientific socialistic publications, Lasalle endeavored to unchain and bring
down to a level with the understanding of the laboring
classes. His keen edged criticism he tries, above all,
on the so-called iron law of wages, which he defines
in the following words: "There is an iron law,
which orders that the wages for the laboring classes,
should, like the oscillations of the pendulum, always
move around and about the lowest point of what may
even yet be sufficient for the necessaries of life required
by the customary standard of life. When wages are higher,
then more marriages are contracted and more children are
born, and the competition of such as look for work, will
in a short time reduce wages again to the least possible
rate. When wages are lower a certain number of people
have to perish on account of insufficient nourishment, so
that while the supply is diminishing the demand for working forces causes wages to increase; consequently wages
can never move away, for a long period, from the lowest
limit of what is required for the maintenace of life."
When *Bastiat Schulze* objected to this definition and asserted that capital-profit was composed of the wages for
privations of the managers of a business, Lasalle replied
in the following pointed sarcastic words: "What! Gain
of capital wages of privations! European millionaires,
ascetics, Hindoo penitents, pillar saints who stand on

one leg on a pillar, extending, with out-stretched arms,
bent-over body and pale features, a plate to the people in
order to collect the reward for their self-denials! This is
the real condition of society! How was it possible for
me to ignore it? But, joking aside! While capital is that
sponge which absorbs all product of labor and the sweat
of the workman, and leaves to the laborer merely the
necessaries of life, you have the hardihood to present to
the workingmen the revenues of capital as a recompense
for privations of capitalists!" The objection that in
the sphere of economy each one was the manufacturer of
his own fortune or misfortune, and consequently was
alone to be held responsible for his condition; Lasalle
meets with a reference to the fatalistic influence of
conjunctures, of the tie of social connections, of that
chain, which combines all existing unknowable circumstances. "The economic sphere," he continues, "distinguishes itself from the juridical by that little difference, that in the former, in our days, everyone is responsible for what he has *not* done, while in the latter, everybody has to answer for what he has done. Fortune plays
ball with the supposed liberty of the individual, thrown
upon his own resources; in this game, which unknown,
and for this reason, uncontrolable powers play with him,
the one is snatched high up into the bosom of wealth,
while hundreds of others are thrown into the deep abyss

of poverty.   The wheel of social coherencies runs over them, their exertions, dilligence and labor, crushing and reforming the same."

Now, in order to remove these evil circumstances, Lasalle demands the displacing of the capitalistic mode of production by means of a system, which would secure to each economic subject a more just distribution of the net national income.   This, however, he does not expect to be achieved unless by subsidiary measures taken by the state.   " It is only necessary," says he in this respect, " to do away with those individual advances, out of which the transfer of the result of production, and the assignment of all surplusses over the necessaries of life are made to the capitalist.   Labor of society, mutual and common anyhow, must be prosecuted by the common mutual advances of the same, and the result of production is to be distributed among all who have participated therein, to each, according to the measure of this work.   The most easy transitory medium to accomplish this will be found in *productive associations of laborers*, hence these associations must be, will be, even if the world should burst." But as the workmen are not in possession of the necessary capital, that being in the hands of the capitalists, the state is to make the required advances, while the associations have to form an organic union.   In order, however, to obtain this assistance from the state, it will be necessary for the laborers first, to gain influence over the government, by means of political representations in the parliaments, to bring about these social reforms. This being obtained, capital would become a dead, unfruitful instrument, subordinated to labor, the only standard of value. The solidarity of labor would at once remove the social misery, and, as the entire laboring class had become enterprisers, each one would receive the full value of his work.

The great activity of Lasalle reacted on Marx, who, from his standpoint, could not approve of the detail arrangements proposed by his energetic contemporary. A short time before Lasalle's death,—he fell in a duel, fought on account of a woman,—Marx had succeeded in forming what is called, " *The Internationale.*" He knew only too well, that his ideal state of the future, would never be organized unless the socialistic movement would become *international.* To make it such, was his constant effort and desire. But in this he would have failed entirely, had not the existing social conditions materially aided him. When, on the floor of the congress of laborers, held at the Haag, *Guillaum,* one of the delegates, remarked, " that the Internationale was the invention of a smart man with an infallible social idea; but, that it was also the product of the surrounding social circumstances," both of these assertions are correct. Marx is without doubt, the founder of that powerful secret association, but various causes had prepared the way for him. One of these was the fact, that the factors of the world-wide ruling system of economy, had become more and more international, especially movable capital. Everywhere the laborers found themselves dependent on, and placed in opposition to the power of free competition, with all its evil consequences. In most of the civilized countries we notice the same contest between capital and labor, the same discontent and class hatred glowing under the surface of society. Hence the silent and expressed desire of the working classes for closer union, even for international solidarity, in order to create a conformable counter pressure against the overwhelming, overpowering, cosmopolitan, unpatriotic capitalism.

The first effort made in this direction, was, perhaps the founding of a laborer association in London, in the year 1840, which comprised German, Hungarian, Polish, Danish, Swedish and English workmen, and which put itself in communication with the Chartistic movement of that time. Out of this union sprang the, "Society of the Fraternal Democrats," which stood in connection with similar societies in France, Belgium and Switzerland. This movement received new impulse in November, 1847, when a body of German Communists met in London. Marx and Engels led the meeting, and in its name, issued a " Manifest," in which the purposes of these Communists were declared, as being perfectly identical with those of all proletarian associations with the only exception, " that they on the one hand defended common interests, inde-- pendent of nationality and of the entire class of the differ- ent national disagreements; and on the other hand, advocated the interests of that common movement through its various stages of development, through which the contest between wage-workers and capitalists had to go." The Manifest closes with the noticeable appeal: " Prole- tarians of all countries, unite." An international congress was appointed for 1848, but the political upheaving of that year, and its final overthrow by state power, for a long time paralized the socialistic movement. It was not before 1862 that it received new life and vigor again. The con- stant increasing economic misery, and extensive strikes, had again brought the working classes of Europe, espec- ially those in England on their feet, and driven them into the political arena. The London Exhibition brought a number of French laborers to that city as delegates, to seek a union with those of England. An exchange of opinions took place and the solidarity of interests of the working classes of the different countries was declared. But it was not until 1864 when Marx succeeded in realiz- ing his fervent desire, "to see a laborer association founded, comprising the most advanced countries of

Europe and America, whose aim and end it should be, bodily to exhibit to the laborers themselves and to the Bourgeoisie and the governments the international character of the socialistic movement for the encouragement and invigoration of the Proletariate, as a terror to its enemies." In that year a great and imposing convocation of laborers from all countries had been called to St. Martins Hall in London. The meeting was opened September 28th, under the presidency of Prof. Beesley. Among the distinguished delegates we notice Mazzini, his private secretary Major Wolf and Marx, who for the first time appeared again on the public arena. After a provisory committee and a General Council had been appointed, a resolution was carried demanding a declaration of principles. Mazzini presented an Inaugural address, together with a Constitution, directed to all the laborers of the civilized society. But as the same was more suitable for a political conspiration - society, than an international socialistic union, the meeting refused the adoption of the address. Marx in the meantime had prepared a Constitution, and an address, both of which were passed by a decided majority. Mazzini withdrew and left Marx sole controller of the proceedings. In 1866 the provisory Constitution of Marx received its sanction on the part of the congress held in Geneva. Very significant are the explanations and the Rationale given in the preamble to

the Constitution, viz.: " The emancipation of the working classes must be achieved by themselves, the contest
for the emancipation of the laboring people does not mean
a combat for class privileges and monopolies, but for
equal rights and duties, and for the abolishment of every
domination of classes. The economic dependency of the
man of labor on the monopolist of the means of labor, the
source of life, signifies the foundation of servitude in every
form of social misery, of the mental degradation and of
political vassalage. For this reason the economic emancipation of the working classes remains the great end to
which every political movement, as a subsidiary means,
must always be subordinated. All societies and individuals, who join the International Laborers Association
acknowledge the principles of truth, justice and morality,
as the rule for their conduct towards each other, and all
men, without regard to color, belief, or nationality; no
duties without rights, no rights without duties.''

Now, it is not my purpose to give you a detailed survey of all the proceedings of the different meetings held
by the Internationale, as long as it stood united, or of the
sectional congresses held since its split in 1872. Such
a review would not be very edifying and agreeable. But
allow me to remark in general that the creation, and the
continuation of the Internationale has been of an immense importance for the spreading of socialistic tenden-

cies.   Since that time Socialism has recorded advances
that are surprising and alarming at the same time.

Of course, the different congresses were held principally for the very purpose of giving to the socialistic
movement an international world-wide basis.   Then the
leaders of the different countries came together in order
to compare notes, to discuss principles, aims and ends,
to harmonize local and national differences of opinions.
Thus, for example, during the second Congress held in
Geneva in 1866, the question was raised whether the
"mental proletariate" was to be counted among the
laborers proper.   Had it not been for the German and
English delegates, the intellectual originator of the Internationale himself, would have been counted out.   Thus,
very often, personal, egotistic contrarieties and an unpleasant mixture of economic and political radicalism
sprung up, and petty rivalries prevented an harmonious
working together, especially since the anarchistic element
has succeeded in getting under its control to a large extent the socialistic current.   Since that time, personal
invectives, harsh denunciations are the order of the day
among the leaders of the fiendish movement.   But in spite
of all that it must be admitted, that the laborers saw in this
association a central point, which gave to their intentions
and efforts the necessary back-bone.   One result the
Internationale has gained already; it has succeeded in

throwing class-hatred, in all countries, as a fire-brand into the working classes, that has set society ablaze. Besides, whatever may be the local, national or personal dissensions, there is an infernal unity of purpose apparent among the different socialistic sections. Very significantly this fundamental harmony is expressed by one of the delegates to the congress in 1873, after a futile attempt had been made to heal the division called forth the year before: "We regret this rupture, as both parties are united in the opinion that labor has to become the reason for a division of society. Strictly taken, only the ways are different, the purposes are one and the same. Our opponents may not triumph on account of this split; wherever it is necessary to confront the ruling class and to defend the right of labor, all socialists are united no matter in which direction they turn." Sufficient proof of this we find in the indubitable fact, that of late the different branches of the original Internationale and the various socialistic sections observe a more methodic advance. They have all stepped out of the stadium of considering principles, into that of actual aggression; and in this they exhibit a wonderful unanimity. Allow me to call your attention to a few facts.

First of all, notice the abundant means that are collected for party purposes in all countries, and directed hither and thither in order to aid in the advancement of

the cause.   Thus, local strikes, or associates, who, in the
course of their agitation may have come in contact with
the prunitive and repressive power of the state are amply
assisted; or by means of such aid, the election of one of
their number into the Reichstag, Parliament, etc., is obtained.   Besides, not only inciting international Manifests
are issued from Geneva, Paris, London or New York,
but numerous revolutionary Apostles also are sent out in
all directions, in order to propagate the cause, to arouse
the conciousness of solidarity among the working classes,
and, if necessary, to urge them to aggressive action.
This secret, disquieting, international activity of Socialism, has been of late established, and proved, beyond a
shadow of doubt, on the occasions of attempted assassinations of Princes, or other displeasing officials, of conspiracies or revolutionary excesses committed here and
there.   In this connection it is also worthy of notice, that
the celebration of memorial datas of revolutionary events,
or of prominent socialistic leaders and agitators, as those
of Lasalle, Marx, Mazzini; or of the dates of socialistic
conspiracies, assassinations, etc., is systematically employed, in order to keep awake the destructive passions of
the masses, and to hold them in readiness for bloody
action, when time demands it.   Thus for example, the
18th of March, as the day of the first insurrection of Socialism, is celebrated by the followers of the party of all

countries. Other events have the prospect of being honored with a like cosmopolitan distinction. By degrees a socialistic festive cyclus of memorable blood-thirsty socialistic persons and events will be formed.

THE AIM AND END OF SOCIALISM.

Now, this brief historical review of the development of Socialism compels me , finally, to state in a concise form the actual aim and end of this present movement.

In doing so I feel constrained to restrict myself to the utterances of Socialism proper, as presented to you in the foregoing investigation, and to pass by the local and individual intentions and tendencies of such, as might be called half-breeds of Socialism. When, for example, *Henry George, Alfred Russel Wallace* and *H. M. Hyndman* insist upon nationalizing ground and soil, but admit all the rights which private capital as a means of production enjoys under the present economic regime, then they may be considered as a socialistic reform party, but never as full-blooded Socialists. Of course it is not our concern, through which different forms of migration, they, especially the first named, may pass before they get entirely settled in their views. This merely *en passant*. Socialism must be judged by itself and from its own expressions.

Now from the foregoing exhibit of its tenets and doctrines, you must have observed that it is an utterly unfounded, though wide-spread charge, Socialism intended an equal communistic division of property. Just the opposite is the fact, as it strives to do away with the individualistic cutting up and maintaining of the means of production. All socialistic parties, however they may differ on some points, unitedly object to all private property and capital, and to every form of laborless income, be it in the shape of land-rent, capital-profit or interest or plus-value. They consider these economic forms and rights of productions, though protected by law, as a gross injustice to labor, the only producer of value; hence they demand the transmutation of private into common or collective property. That is, the means of production are to be taken out of the hands of the individual and placed into the possession of the commonwealth.

There is some difference of opinion among the various socialistic sections, as to the proper interpretation of the fundamental principle, that labor is entitled to the full benefit of its product. As far as this asserted right includes the negation of all laborless income, they are of one mind, but they vary as to its positive function The one side claims for the workman his full portion of the value which he added to the net collective value of the goods produced. This right being established, there would be no further possibility for working capital to appropriate to itself in advance a part of the net gain. The other, more conservative side maintains, that the distribution of the proceeds should be made "according to the reasonable wants of the individual." In other words, they postulate merely the *right to existence*, while the former insists upon the right to a full recompense for labor rendered. Within the limits of these two asserted rights Socialism moves at present.

Another point of difference relates to the question, with whom the title to the collective property in working capital should be vested in the aspired state of the future. That is, it is a matter of discussion yet among the Socialists, " Whether associations of workingmen should be entrusted with the collective property in the means required for their respective production, and should be entitled to a common use thereof; or whether that title should be held by the community, the state or, as the congress of Marseilles wanted it, by the entire human race. Or, is there, perhaps, a combination of these different standpoints to take place, so that, for example, the state, the body politic, would own the productive means, as land and capital, but would allow to the individual or the association, the use and management of the same. On all these points recent socialistic publications and resolutions of socialistic congresses give but indefinite, sometimes contradicting answers." (Menger, p. 104 ff.)

Socialists, therefore, appear perfectly harmonious in their exertion to overturn the existing social order, and

the economic traditionary rights, while their opinions run
apart as soon as the fundamental principles and ideas of
right, which shall form the foundation of the socialistic
state come into consideration. This however, is a fact
that explains itself, as common and universal experience
has shown long ago, that for the purpose of agitation,
persistent criticising of existing conditions is the most
ready and efficient weapon to concentrate the masses,
while practical measures generally cause dissension.
Thus far, of necessity, the strength of Socialism lies in
the direction of denying, calling into question, etc.

As for its positions, the so-called Gotha programme,
adopted by most of the socialistic sections, expresses, perhaps, the same with the greatest precision of form and
contents. As far as general postulates are concerned, its
wording is as follows: "1. Labor is the source of all
wealth and culture, and because, generally, useful labor
is only possible by means of society, therefore to society,
that is, to all its members, belongs the entire product of
labor, together with the duty to work, common to all, and
with equal rights. In the society of the present day,
however, the means of production are the monopolies of
capitalists. The dependence of the working classes, in
consequence of such monopolies, is the cause of misery
and servitude in various forms. Hence the emancipation of labor demands the conversion of the means of

labor into a common good of society, and a fellow
or associate regulating of the entire work, together with
an appropriation of the result of labor, beneficial to all
and with a just distribution of the same.

"2. Based on these principles, the socialistic labor party,.
purposes a free state, a socialistic society, the crushing
of the iron law of wages, the abolishment of fleecing in.
any form or shape, and the removal of all social and political inequalities." . . . "Religion is to be declared
a private matter."

You will perceive from this that the demands and aspirations of the Socialists are of an *economic*, a *political* and
a *religious* nature. The fundamental postulate, however,
is an economic one; because, as Marx asserts, the totality
of the productive conditions or the economic structure of
society forms the real basis, on which rises a juridical
and political superstructure. The method of production
of material life, conditions the social, political and intellectual process of life in general. That is, in other words,.
according to socialistic conceptions, the political, religious and social life of any nation, depends on its method
of production, and its economic standard of life. " When
the economic, fundamental conditions of society are revo-
lutionized, then also the juridical, civil, moral and aesthet-
ic, etc., superstructure will change; respectively, break
down," thus writes the editor of the " Neue Gesellschaft."

Now, in as much as Socialism intends a total change of economic order, laws and regulations, it will be seen at once, that the *civil* and *political* alterations will and must be just as radical and total.   For, when the individualistic method of production, and free competition is to be done away with, then the state or the community must organize labor.   But whereas the internationalizing of this regulation of labor on the part of the body politic, is the primary condition for the realization of the socialistic society, the projected state of the future cannot assume the form of a monarchy, or of a republic, in the accepted sense of the word ; neither can it be national, it has to be either socialistic-international, or nothing at all.

Of the same thoroughness will be the changes in the sphere of religion and the Church.   It is true the above programme declares religion a private matter, and thus gives to itself the appearance as if, from principle, no objection was to be made to the practice of religion.   But inasmuch as the entire economic system of Socialism is rooted in the purest Naturalism, and seeks the grossest Materialism, it evidently follows from that alone, that it is, and must be in its inmost nature, the negation of all religion and religious manifestations.   If Socialism does not mean to put itself in opposition to itself, it cannot allow even a forbearing of religion.   Thanks to God that in this respect socialistic literature and journalism has not for a moment left us in doubt, as will be seen in our subsequent lecture. Taking all together, the aim and end of Socialism is not, a gradual reform of existing evils, or the contemplation of improvements in the economic, political and religious conditions. Socialism simply means a total, complete overthrow of all present order and regulation of society.—Revolution, therefore, is the characteristic signature of the present socialistic movement. From this standpoint we shall subject it to a candid criticism in our next lecture.

LECTURE IV.

A CRITIQUE OF SOCIALISM.

In the last lecture, Socialism presented itself to us as an entirely new conception of the world and the things in it. While it adopts the principles and results of the liberal national economy previously considered, it draws entirely different conclusions from the identical premises. Based on the very same egotism which controls the system of free competition, it yet points out to it a completely reverted direction.

Socialism, you will have observed, does not mean to be a natural improved outgrowth from existing circumstances, but a new plant never known before. It appeared to us as "Atheism in religion, as Democratic-Republicanism in politics, as Collectivism in National Economy, and, we may add, as unbounded optimism in Ethics, as an effort to loosen the family and marriage tie in the home," etc. (Schaffle.) In short, Socialism is to be considered as a revolutionizing system which intends to recast society in all its relations.

Now in criticising this stupendous scheme, let me re-mark at the very outset, that we have to guard against two very common mistakes made up to our time with refer-ence to the character and the purpose of Socialism. Very often intentions and acts are charged to it that are in no wise due to it; or people fail to look at its various aspects as upon inseparable combined features of its very essence. Thus, for example, the opinion is prevalent among common and uncommon people, that the aim and end of Socialism was merely an equal dividing up of all existing wealth and the means of production. The oppo-site has been demonstrated in the previous lecture. In like manner the daily press and the public in general, is ever ready to charge every disturbance and tumult caused by the laboring classes to socialistic agitation.

It is true, that the professed and paid socialistic instiga-tors are only too eager to get a hand into every muddle that promises a gain for their ranks. But at the same time, the fact is not to be overlooked, that as long as the different economic strata of society have been formed, a suppressed resentment has ever existed and at times taken vent in open outbreaks.

On the other hand an equally serious mistake is made when Socialism is merely considered in its economic and political aspects. Its religious phase cannot be separated from the former, as they are in fact, but the logical results of its religious position.

In the following it will be my endeavor, sine ira et *studio*, to review Socialism in the light of its own history and avowed principles, as well as in that of the Word of Light. The enemy of Christianity is entitled to the same candor and impartiality which its friend and supporter receives.

It has been well said that each error has, as a rule, a grain of truth in it, which renders it all the more fascinating and dangerous. The same is true in regard to Socialism which, it must be acknowledged, has its favorable sides. To ignore the same would be indeed a great folly. Thus, for example, even the most decided opponent of Socialism must admit that its founders and defenders, more than anybody else, have exposed and brought to the notice of society the disastrous consequences of the system of free competition. The illustrations and verifications furnished in this respect by Marx, Engels, Lasalle and others have never been refuted. Even in such instances where they have exaggerated or passed one-sided judgment upon existing conditions, their incriminating charges against the social and economic circumstances are not altogether void of every foundation. Besides, Socialism has rendered great service to society by tracing the existing economic differences to their proper source, furnishing incontrovertible evidence that the material condition of the individual is for the greatest part conditioned by the unavoidable consequences of the system of free competition, especially by those of the current private right. Very pertinently says Lasalle in this respect: "The ethical idea of the Burgeoisie is this, that exclusively nothing else but the setting to work of his own powers was to be guaranteed to the individual. If all the people were equally strong, equally educated, equally rich, this idea could be considered as a sufficient and moral one. But as we are not and cannot be, this thought is not sufficient and must of necessity in its consequences lead to grave immorality; for it causes the stronger, better educated and richer to skin and pocket the weaker." Ratzinger, p. 394, 3.

Furthermore, it must meet the approval of every right-thinking mind, when Socialism protests against the conception of the existing capitalistic order of things, as of unalterable laws of nature; and insists that the rights deduced from them by the liberal system, are by no means valid for all time to come. Lasalle has indeed secured to himself a lasting place in juridical philosophy, by showing the fallacy of the reasoning on the part of the defenders of the capitalistic system; and by proving convincingly that the acquired rights are merely historical categories, which, in the course of time, "by the public spirit of progressive development," may be modified or even abolished entirely.

It is also a great advance, and a step in the right direction, when Socialism advocates the necessity of bringing the laborers into a closer union with capital, the laboring force with the productive means. It is unquestionably the greatest curse under which society at present, especially the working classes, are suffering, that capitalism has succeeded in completely separating these indispensable factors of industry from each other.

Socialism insists upon the reuniting of the two, and every unbiased mind must consider this demand as a just one, though we may strongly condemn the measures proposed to bring about such a change. Of equal importance is the fact that Socialism asserts the principle of solidarity of social interests against the abstract individualism of the school of Smith and Ricardo. According to the latter the excellency of any economic system consists in a constantly increasing production, while Socialism more correctly lays the greatest stress on the just and equal distribution of the net proceeds of labor.

Lastly it will admit of no doubt, that the Socialistic conception of the functions of the state as of a cultural institution bound to advance also the ethical, economic and social moments of the life of its subjects, is by far preferable to that of the physiocrats according to whom, in the language of Lasalle, " The purpose of the State is exclusively to protect the personal liberty and property of the individual."

As for the *demands* which Socialism puts to the present Society, it must be confessed that most of them are not only not objectionable, but, in full harmony with the principles of justice and equity. Thus when, without a single exception, all the socialistic sections insist upon the abolishment of children's work in factories, and demand a restriction and proper control of the employment of married women in the manufacturing places, none but selfish and heartless capitalists can object to such a request in general. There may be individual cases, and local circumstances, that may render the employment of women and children in industry for a time unavoidable; but not only the publications of Socialists, but also those of philanthropists, economists and official persons have established the fact long ago, that a transfer of these weaker elements of Society out of their proper sphere into the turmoil of industry, works disastrously on the harmonious development of these individuals as well as on society in general.

To mention a second demand of Socialism: the abolishment of all Sunday work, is it not to the discredit of so-called Christian employers and their religious profession, that they had, and still have to be reminded by the enemies of the Word of God, that there is such a thing as the Fourth Commandment!   Who did not feel the piercing sting of the accusation, couched in the language of an appeal, made by a socialistic Section,—the Baker's Union No. 1—to the clergy of New York only a few weeks ago, when it gives utterance to the following words: "We are not only compelled to work long hours every day, but a great number of our comrades are compelled to work even on Sunday, the natural day of rest and re-creation.   This, we believe, should not be; but all attempts on our part to have Sunday work abolished were of no avail.   We therefore appeal to the clergy of this city for assistance.   We beseech you, Reverend Gentlemen, to do all in your power to have this nuisance abolished within your respective parishes; and, as we hold that your duty as clergymen and humanitarians commands you to see that the Sabbath Day is not desecrated by toil, we feel satisfied that our appeal to you will not have been made in vain."

Thus, it will be seen that there is even more than a mere grain of truth in the system under consideration. Besides, it is admitted on all sides, that Socialism indi-rectly has produced very salutary effects upon the public mind, as well as upon social science.   The constantly multiplying socialistic issues, and the indomitable agita-

tion of the leaders, have called the attention of high and
low, of the church as well as of the state; in short, of
everybody concerned about the welfare of others, to the
social question in its various relations and issues. As a
beneficial result of this general interest taken in the
matter, there must be mentioned, on the one side, the fact
that sociology of late has experienced a wholesome
change. The so-called realistic-positive school represented by men like Wagner, Schaffle, Lange, Ihring,
Schonberg, Held and others, has reduced the socialistic
charges against capitalism to their proper limits; put
the claims and the boasts of Socialism in their due light,
and is putting forth unceasing efforts to introduce into
economics sound and Christian principles. On the other
hand, the persistent tenacious onslaught of Socialism
against the present order of Society, has aroused the
statesmen and governments of all civilized nations to a
legislative and executive activity in the sphere of social
reforms never before witnessed to such a degree. In
spite of the opposition on the part of Liberalism and
Capitalism inside and outside the Halls of Legislation and
governmental chambers, social and economic measures
have been initiated, and are still in progress of introduction, that have not only proved a blessing to the trodden-
down classes, but have done more to counteract socialistic agitation than all exceptional repressive laws and

acts put together. The policy of Bismarck and his supporters, for example, has of late been so thoroughly social with reference to the alleviation of the economic evils, that it has been stigmatized by its opponents as State Socialism.

The church also is awakening to its duty, and begins to take an active part in the discussions of the needs and wants of the laboring classes, and of the proper means to remove the glaring evils in society.

Now, all this and perhaps still more, may safely be said in favor of Socialism without in the least coming in conflict with truth and reality. But it will be seen at once that its merit thus far, exists merely in negation and criticism, which indeed may be of great value in its proper place; but, as Socialism proposes an entire reconstruction of the present order of things, it must be able to convince us of its excellency and preferableness. But in this respect, Socialism not only fails completely, but suggests social and economic measures, which, when carried into effect, would prove a disaster to mankind, religiously and socially considered. Let me substantiate this assertion by a few considerations:

Socialism when compared with Liberalism in the ruling system of economy, seems to be the exact counterpart of the latter, and yet a closer examination of it, reveals the startling fact that Socialism, as well as the system of

Smith, Ricardo, etc., spring from one common source, namely, from *Materialism*, and *Atheism*. Some well-disposed and even Christian people have expressed the opinion "That the Socialist; purely out of expediency, turned to Atheism, and because the Materialistic drift of our time made it necessary for him. But that the system itself did not necessitate it." (Todt.) Socialists themselves, however, protest against such an interpretation of their religious position. Marx, for example, writes in "Den deutch franzoesischen Jahrbuechern," p. 73, the following: "The root for man is man himself. The evident proof for the Radicalism of the German theory, consequently also for its practical energy is its proceeding from the decided, positive abolishment of religion. A criticism of religion ends with the doctrine *that man is the highest being for man;* consequently, with the categorical imperative to overthrow all conditions in which man is a degraded, enslaved, forsaken and detested being; which circumstances cannot be described any better than by the exclamation of a Frenchman, when a dog-tax was projected, 'Poor dogs, they are going to treat you like men.'" Another one writes: "It must be publicly stated that only the Materialistic, perhaps better, the Monistic view of the world, as it is confirmed more and more by modern science, coincides with the principles of Socialism, and gives to it that broad basis on

which they can rear themselves as a complete superstructure.''

Now out of this Atheistic conception of things very naturally flows the *Materialistic tendency* which characterizes
the Socialistic system.   As man in Socialistic theology is
the highest being for himself, we can well understand the
fact that in the economic system of this school, the individual is made the starting point, as well as the end, of all
its propositions and movements.   While Socialism seem-
ingly opposes with energy and bitterness the individualism in capitalism, it endeavors to establish and invest
individualism with supreme power; for in Socialism the
ideal state of the future, or society in general, is merely
intended and projected in order to use it as a means for
the realization of the interests and desires of the individual.   Even the looseness of thought expressed with reference to the sanctity and integrity of family ties and relations, finds its ready explanation in the individualistic
liberalism of Socialism.

We do not wonder, therefore, in the least, that Marx
deduced from this alleged position of man an unquestion-
able right to subvert all orders of Society which seem to
prevent the individual from enjoying his eminent, social
prerogatives.   The *religious* Radicalism of Socialism,
peremptorily demands the political, that is the absolute
right, in a summary way, to supplant the existing rules

and regulations of the commonwealth, by the Atheistic, Materialistic state of the future. Since Socialism professedly is done with the "Idea of God," it cannot but attempt to eradicate all social and economic arrangements which claim to have been developed by Divine permission, and from that fact deduce their relative title to existence.

Now, it is this very religious radicalism underlying and giving energy to the socialistic movement, that must call out the most decided opposition on the part of a sound Christian conception of things. Even if we would for a moment suspend our specific Christian judgment, the indubitable fact that an atheistic, materialistic commonwealth never has and never will exist, must turn our hearts and minds against the proposed irreligious, socialistic order of society.

Besides, a system that knows and seeks but material interests, puts itself in direct opposition to the eternal purpose of God with man, and also to the vital interests of society itself. For man very far from being the object of himself is rather created to God, and whenever he attemps to subvert this, his Divine ordination, he thereby prepares for himself, and all his undertakings the way to certain destruction. Socialism may for a time tyrannize humanity, and I do not know whether it will not be that form of political, social and economic rule that is to precede the coming of the Son of Man in glory. (Read

for example II. Thess. 2, and Rev. 17–19.) But just as
sure as it is of necessity anti-christian in its spirit and
tendency, it stands condemned by the Word of Truth, as
well as by history and human experience. An examination of its proposed economical superstructure will lead
us to an equally rejecting judgment.

And here allow me to say in general, that Socialism
makes a serious mistake in setting aside entirely the duty
of connecting its reformatory efforts, with what has developed itself in the course of history, and exists at present in the form of acquired rights. Socialism, as we
noticed in our previous lecture, does not believe in a
reformation of the existing economic evils. On the contrary it makes every effort to increase the same to an
unbearable degree, in order then to obtain the necessary
power for that well-planned revolution, that is to overthrow the present order of things. There are, indeed,
such in the ranks of Socialists, who disown any and every
anarchistic plotting on their part, especially since the
recent, well remembered, anarchistic cruelties in Belgium,
Chicago, etc. But official, as well as unofficial issues,
even of these moderate socialists, confirm the opinion that
for the present, only prudential reasons dictate such a
moderation. They know but too well that every unsuc-
cessful, untimely brawl must injure their cause. Besides,
the repressive and punitive power of the State is, as yet,

too energetic, that they should imprudently expose themselves to its iron grasp and hold. Otherwise, there is no
doubt that Socialists, as well as Anarchists, heartily sub-
scribe to that part of the manifest which the *Wydener* Congress issued in August, 1880: "The crushing majority
of German Social-Democrats, never gave itself over to the
illusion that they would be able to carry their principle
into effect in a peaceful manner, in the purely legal way.
That is, that the privileged classes, voluntarily and without
coercion would give up their advantageous position. But
that we ever should abandon the carrying out of our
principles in case the ruling classes should cut off every
"legal" way, no German Socialist ever thought of such a
thing; and it has been understood from the beginning, that
in this case, which according to historical experience must
be anticipated, *every means* must be right and justifiable.
—If matters do not bend from above they must break up-
ward from below." That is certainly plain language.

But this very revolutionary tendency of socialism calls
forth the severest criticism. Aside from the fact that this
refractory spirit is the very opposite of the spirit breath-
ing through the sacred pages, it must be maintained, that
the social and economical circumstances, though they be
extremely sad, are by no means beyond the reach of amelioration. On the contrary during the last two decades, in
all social, civil and economic spheres, there is noticed an

unmistakable activity and energy to bring about a more satisfactory, peaceful state of affairs, and it can not be denied that on the whole these efforts have to a great extent been crowned with a lasting success. The necessity of drawing the boundaries of individualistic capitalism closer, is freely acknowledged; and thousands of well-meaning minds, are earnestly at work to secure a more equal distribution of the national wealth. Now while these remedial measures are proposed and introduced, it is certainly criminal conduct on the part of the avowed Socialist, to attempt to check this progress merely for the sake of being better enabled to obtrude a preposterous scheme upon mankind.

Of the same character is the internationalizing of things and people as advocated by Socialism. For nations as well as nationalities are Divinely ordered, ruled and governed organisms which, in the great world-drama and especially for the realization of the Kingdom of God have to perform a Divinely-ordained part. It is true according to distinct promises of the Word of Life, and the general expectation of the Church of the Redeemer, based on those promises, the nations of the earth shall be transformed into a higher unit. But that unit is certainly not to be looked for in the proposed compulsory, economical leveling, that Socialism dreams of, but in the consummation of the kingdom of the Son of Man.

Socialism is equally perverse in simply rejecting the individualistic principle of the school of Smith-Ricardo, instead of modifying it   While its criticism of the same stands proof in general, it seriously errs in demanding its entire suppression.   Since *private* production in its absoluteness has created so many evils, Socialism feels warranted in attempting to supplant it by collective or common production.   But here it entirely overlooks the significant fact that both of these factors in economy have co-existed together by common consent, as well as by law; and that the economic private interest has constantly been of the greatest importance to collective or common interest.   Society, therefore, is not shut up to the alternative whether a private or Socialistic method of production is to be introduced.   There is still the other question to be considered: How economical individualism can be regulated so as to insure alongside, and in union with common production, the greatest possible and just distribution of the national income, among the constituent parts of any commonwealth.   Unfortunately this question is never asked by Socialism.

Passing over to the essential feature of Socialism, you will remember that its principal demand is the abolishing of private property as a means of production, and its conversation into collective or common property.   In support of this position two reasons are advanced: 1. It is asserted that private property, as capital, is the source of all social and economic misery; hence the necessity of doing away with it. 2. Society-labor is the only producer of value; hence private capital is actually only "wages," taken away by it from the wage-earner. Consequently private capital is to be abrogated, and the proceeds of labor must be owned and possessed entirely by Society,—that is the laborers.

Now, as to the first reason our review of the workings of the system of free competition has convinced us, that the absolute use and employment of private capital, as practiced and sanctioned by that system, has many misdeeds to account for. We have also admitted, that most of the charges of Socialism against individualistic capitalism are only too well founded. But thus far, Socialism has failed to prove the utter impossibility to remedy these evils. But as long as it is not able to do so, its demand to abolish private capital on that ground is, to say the least, unjust. There is certainly nothing in the nature of private capital itself, nor in the expression of God's Word on its relation to man and heavenly things, nor in its historic development as a potent factor in economy, nor in the established right and law of Society, nor in sound and equitable social principles that would and could stamp the use and employment of productive capital, an intolerable wrong, peremptorily

to be removed. On the contrary private capital is
recognized in the Word of God, sanctioned by common,
universal consent and usage from time memorial, and protected by right and law of all civilized nations. As for
its evil workings, it partakes of the general corruption and
imperfection of all earthly things and relations, for which,
however, an efficient remedy has been provided. Alas,
the irreligious Radicalism of Socialism prevents it from
adopting and applying that Divinely appointed remedy.

Equally baseless is its second reason for the up-rooting
of a long established, economic institute. For the assertion that capital was nothing but the curdled wages unjustly taken from the laborer, is too absolutely and ab-
stractly made. Even when we admit, as we must, that
under the present economic order and rights of society,
capital will always obtain the advantage over labor, we
are very far from drawing the same conclusion from this
fact that Socialism chooses to draw from it. For even
under the rule and reign of the present system, the possibility is not excluded to fix more justly and to greater
satisfaction, that share which capital and labor respectively may rightly claim for itself in the net income of
production. But as long as such a possibility is extant,
there is no just cause to abrogate private capital, together
with the system of paying wages. It is true that it will
be exceedingly difficult, nay absolutely impossible in

general, as well as in every specific case, to fix exactly to
the dollar, or cent, the claim which the one or the other
of these two prominent factors of production may rightly
raise;—that would be just as impossible under the reign
of the socialistic system.   Nevertheless general principles
may be laid down and carried into effect by means of
which the evident tendency of capitalism to take advantage of the laborer, would be restrained, and the gradation of wages might be brought into a more just relation
to labor and its exertions.

Of course this reply is based on the supposition that
capital, as a distinct and indispensable factor of production, is as such entitled to some reward.   But this is what
Socialism denies, by maintaining that only labor is to be
regarded as the producer of value.   It expressly avers:
"Thus Labor, the producer, is naturally also the owner
of the total value.   Collective labor contains the labor
of the individuals, these therefore are, as producers also
owners of the entire value.   Whatever of these different
values may be productive means or capital, becomes
possession of society; and whatever is a means for enjoyment, is apportioned to each workman according to the
measure of the average labor of society."

Now, you will at once perceive the one-sidedness and
sophistry forming the basis of this assertion.   For every
person of sound mind will rightly maintain, that besides

labor there are other factors in economy that create value. In this connection I mention merely *nature* and *want*. Marx indeed declares: "The same quantity of labor exhibits itself, the season of the year being favorable, in eight bushels of wheat that during an unfavorable season four bushels represent." "Diamonds," he further asserts, "are seldom found in the ground, and their discovery therefore, on an average requires much labor; consequently they represent in a small volume, a large amount of labor." But these very examples show us the sophistry with which this mental founder of Socialism tries to substantiate his theory as to the value created by labor alone. For, in the first place, it is simply not true that those four bushels required the same amount of labor as the eight. The time for tilling and sowing may be equal in both cases, but it is certainly not as far as reaping and preparing are concerned. There the four bushels represent a less quantity of labor, and according to the Socialistic idea, they ought to bring therefore, a lower price per bushel in the market, having cost less labor.

As for the diamonds, we meet with the same fallacy. For the price of these is not at all in proportion to their scarcity, or to the amount of labor expended on them. There are, as everybody is aware, very scarce minerals that man cares nothing about. Why then does he look for diamonds at all? And why does he value them at a price that stands in no relation to the amount of work caused in their discovery? Unless we are greatly mistaken there are other considerations which take part in the fixing of the price of these specific minerals. It is therefore nothing but sheer sophistry that Marx is guilty of, when he presumes to support his favorite idea as to the producer of value by such and numerous other invalid examples.

The entire argumentation of Socialism very strangely proceeds on the silent pre-supposition, that the projected socialistic order of things has been inaugurated already. Then of course, it would, in the language of the notorious John Most, make not the slightest difference, whether, "In two different farming districts, on an equally large area and by the employment of the same number of laborers, and the same utensils, entirely different proceeds should be achieved." For, Most continues, " if with regard to ground and soil collective property exists, then the question is not how much here and how much there has been realized, but only what the proceeds of the entire country are, because the laborers would participate in that, and not in the produce of each separate section." That is, in other words, Most admits indirectly, that besides labor there are other causes which contribute value to a thing; but unfortunately they cannot be admit-

ted in the socialistic state of the future. Hence the correctness of the Socialistic theory as to value depends
entirely on the realization of the ideal, novel order of
things: othererwise it is utterly untenable and could not
be carried into effect under any other method of production. For as long, as for example, it is admitted that there
is such a thing as a *natural* value, a value furnished by
nature independent of labor or exertion, so long this
natural value must be permitted together with labor to
share in the proceeds of production. Take for an instance,
the raw material, *wool*, which by means of labor is converted into *yarn*. In this raw material, the owner possesses an article of demand, composed of value, contrib-
uted to it, partly by nature and partly by labor. Now,
when he hands this valuable article over to the general
process of production, then, an object is created which
in its new form possesses a greater value than that which
it could command in its previous state. Now the question arises whether that labor which created this plus
value is exclusively entitled to claim it as its own, or
whether to the natural value attaching to the raw material,
there is also due a share in the final market price of the
produced article ? Socialism replies to the first question
in the affirmative, to the second in the negative, while sound
reason reverts the answer. For, even admitted, that the
owner of the wool, by giving it over to the general process

of manufacturing, seeks his own interest, it cannot be denied that by doing so he also initiates for the benefit of the community a series of activities, calculated to create new and additional values. For this philanthropic action he, as the owner of the raw material, or of the natural value thereof, is certainly entitled to a part of the net gain. The personal risk which the owner assumes, and his ordering, directing, watching co-operation, I do not even mention ; though both of them are incalculable elements in the manufacturing process. Taking all together, we are driven to the conclusion, that, of all theories advanced with reference to the formation of value the socialistic is the most absurd and unjust. The fault lies not in the things themselves, but in the one-sided definition which socialism chooses to give to them. But we turn to another subject.

Rodbertus, in a certain place, calls the book of Marx on capital an "invasion into human society." Of the fundamental socialistic demand, it may be said with equal pertinency, that it is an invasion into personal liberty, and human rights. Take as an illustration and proof its position in regard to *private property*. It simply denies the same, and that in the face of the significant fact, that individual property as a means of production has been recognized alongside of common or society-property, not only among civilized, but also among uncivilized nations, and that as long as any commonwealth has been formed. The ethnological and anthropological works of men like Peschel, Waitz and others furnish sufficient proof to this fact. Private property therefore, is a universal historical category; but it is more than that: it has also assumed the form of a juridical institute, that is, by universal custom and usage, as well as by express enactments, it has been recognized, defined and circumscribed or extended. But this uniform and universal formation and development of private property, is by no means a matter of arbitrariness, but is founded in conclusive reasons. Of course, man as a social being is entitled to the enjoyment of the means for his support. But when common universal custom, as well as the law of every land, conveys to him the indefeasable title to private productive means, then such an important grant can have its reason only in the fact, that society discovered in this social and economic right and order, the surest guarantee for the satisfaction of the legitimate self-interest of the individual as well as for the attainment of the greatest possible welfare of the commonwealth. At the same time, in the fixing of the individual or private right regard was always paid to the claims which the first occupation of derelict property, or the first cultivation of the same presented. Now, all this goes to show that private property is a legal institution, which ought not to be abrogated unless individual and common interest peremptorily demands such abolishment. The latter Socialism indeed asserts; but thus far it has failed to furnish stringent proofs for such an averment. Even when we admit, that, in consequence of the reign of capitalistic individualism, and the deleterious influence of the Roman law, an absolute conception of private property has obtained sanction and authority, which cannot stand either before the forum of Christian principles nor of society interests, —even, when as a result of this creeping in of a wrong idea, oppressive social and economic evils have arisen— still these facts do not call for a subversion of the existing right and order of private property. There is, as yet, a possibility of a modification of the abstract conception of property, and of a corresponding change of the economic disparity. If therefore Socialism by means of revolution and force, attempts the overthrow of the present form of right and law, then it undertakes an unjustifiable attack on the historical development and the legal confirmation of the right to private property, and thereby on individual rights sanctioned and guaranteed by the state.

In addition to this, Socialism deceives its own adherents by affirming, that, by means of the transmutation of private into collective capital, the putrid source of egotism would forever be covered up, and every possibility of taking advantage be removed. It is indeed more than folly, in the face of an almost six thousand years' experience of mankind to the very contrary, to expect us to believe that a radical change of the social and economic basis of society, would work a still greater change in the moral tendency of human nature which finds vent in egotism. Even though *Cabet*, the French socialist, declares: "When we are asked: 'What is your science?' We answer, 'Fraternity!' 'What is your theory?' 'Fraternity!' 'What is your doctrine?' 'Fraternity!' 'What is your system?' 'Fraternity!''" —we are still too skeptic to expect such a wonderful result from a mere shifting of material potencies. For if the Word of Life be true, then nothing short of God's almighty grace is able to subdue and root out that sinful selfishness which causes so much strife and bitterness among men. Besides, thus far the internal history of Socialism itself, and its external unwarranted brutal attacks on existing rights and order, are anything but calculated to inspire us with implicit confidence in the benign results avowedly incident to the realization of its projected scheme. For if the tree must be judged by its fruit, society has every reason to pray: Lord preserve us from the vandalism of Socialism.

As for the ideal state of the future, Schaffle very truly says: "The delusion that in the Socialistic state of democratic, collective production, door and gate would be barred against every 'fleecing' is perfectly vain. It is

true the private capitalist could not take any more advantage of wage labor, for private capital would be dismant-
led. But the laborer would be in a condition thoroughly
to drain the co-laborer. The same would be true of the
directing and the directed, of the lazy and the conscientious, of the bold and the timid co-producer, of the
demagogue and his opponent. While the quantitative
controling of the time of labor, the fixing of the normal
achievement of work, the computation of intensive into
extensive work was going on, things might be practiced
that would allow the cipitalistic vampyre of Marx to
appear as a respectable figure when compared with the
social democratic parasites, demagogues and majority-
drones." (Aussichtslosigkeit, p. 33.)

Above all, there is in social life a self-interest which
finds Divine recognition in the words, " As thyself " in
the second great command of our Master. Of course it is
to take its impetus, as well as its direction and limit, from
the motive of the first and highest command—the love
to God. By means of this self-interest in the acquiring
and managing of private capital, personal as well as common advantages have been achieved, which deserve the
greatest credit. But what the result would be if by abolishing all individual interest, the limits for economic self-
activity should be fixed indefinitely the history of all previous communistic undertakings has sufficiently foretold.

But we pass on in order to glance at the exercise of the right of *personal liberty*, as it would take shape or form in the state of the future. If we could trust the affirmation of the socialistic leaders, then the golden age would dawn upon the world in that very respect. But as long as logic is logical, it is as clear as sunlight, that Socialism must sacrifice personal liberty, if it maintains, as it does, social equality. Under the present system the individual possesses the right of migration and of emigration—and immigration in order to secure his economical purposes. But what would be the case in the socialistic state? Its collective production would have to be managed even in its details by state-supervision, and that according to the wants of the people, ascertained and determined by official statistics. Each economic individual would have to submit willingly or unwillingly to the power and whims of the official need or want. Migration, or the right to look anywhere for a source of obtaining a livelihood, would be impossible. Neither could the individual enjoy the privilege of choosing under all circumstances his own profession. It is true, even now, not everybody selects just that occupation or trade because he desires it above every other one. Very often, as is the case with miners, Providence has cast the lot of certain persons into a region that sustains itself by mining; or the son follows the steps or dictates of his father. Sometimes external family or economic circumstances are decisive in the selection of a comparatively more onerous and dangerous calling. In other words, man is very often constrained by the power of external conditions. But as in the socialistic state, the consciousness of *perfect social equality* would be raised to its highest pitch, such regards for and submissions to determining contingencies would not hold out. Why should anyone choose for example mining, when he discovers in himself the physical and mental material for a merchant, or even for something higher than that. But onerous and detestable work must be done; that is, in other words, in collective production the socialistic state must apply force—must command. " But whether a population grown up under the present economic conditions would bear such a tyranny of the state, is very questionable; because man submits to the power of circumstances, and reconciles himself to them; but the power of the state which has become to him the power of arbitrariness,he will hate." (Truempelmann).

Of a still more delusive character is the socialistic promise of *social, economic equality.* The national economy of the physiocrats and the school of Smith and Ricardo demanded the equal title to personal and economic traffic or *equal rights.* Of course it did not for a moment think of asking also for the equality of social and economic conditions. Socialism, however, more consequent, has in all earnestness made this demand, and promised for the state of the future "That every political and social inequality would be abrogated therein." Now, it will be easily understood that the lower classes hail such a promise with rejoicing; and are putting forth every energy speedily to initiate that happy time. But when we take the liberty to scrutinize the socialistic expectation, we soon discover a significant uncertainty as to how this equality is to be taken. There is especially a decided diversity of opinion, with reference to the proper standard to be fixed for the distribution of the collective income. The majority, as we demonstrated in our former lecture, is of the opinion that each economic individual ought to be remunerated according to the measure of normal or society labor rendered, because, they say, an indiscriminate indemnification of labor would blunt every aspiration; certainly very true. The minority, however, considers a richer endowment and qualification, even the greater activity of the one as a "product of nature," for which the individual does not deserve an extra gratification. That is, the minority finds itself in entire harmony with the atheistic, materialistic view, giving life and energy to the socialistic system. For, if man is but a product of nature, as for example the leaf on the tree, then of course neither the less qualified laborer, nor even the lazy-bone is to be blamed if he does not accomplish as much as those better endowed. Why should he then suffer for what nature has simply failed to supply? The minority undoubtedly has logic in its favor provided the premises are well founded.

Thus we see, that Socialism itself is at a loss how to bring about the economic equality which it has made the very corner-stone of its system. This is perhaps the reason why the above-mentioned Gotha-programme demands the distribution in question, according to the "reasonable wants" of the individual. But, take either of these three proposed methods, and you will find that the one is as impossible and absurd as the other. As to the first, or the demand that labor rendered should form the only basis for the distribution of the collective income, even the socialist ought to have sense enough to see the extreme difficulty to determine, what would form the standard or normal working-time, by which each individual labor was to be measured. But even when, by extensive observations, and by means of obligatory statistics, the general labor bureau should succeed in fixing, to the satisfaction of all, the necessary average time for each work and each kind of work, it would still find itself utterly unable to define the exact portion which each individual workman, or class of artisans, had added to the market value of the goods produced. By what standard, for example, should the respective part which the originating, designing, calculat-

ing, directing and combining mind has taken in the production of goods, be measured ?   Or which master-mind
would be able to determine precisely the relation which
each of the numerous particles of time of the heterogene-
ous workmen would sustain to the indivisible value which
they jointly have created ? Certainly Socialism would have
to settle this and many other difficulties, either by peremp-
tory decision, or as capitalism does by mutual agreement
of the parties interested.   But where in either case would
be the fulfillment of the promise that labor should receive
its full value ?

   That the second method indicated is even less accept-
able, Socialism itself has proved by its extensive opposition to it.   But if the third should be introduced, how
quickly would the " reasonable wants," of each particle
of the sovereign socialistic people be cultivated to such a
degree, that the directors of the collective world production would be amazed and perplexed.   If Socialism was not
determined wilfully to shut its eyes against certain facts
connected with its history, it would have been convinced
long ago that even among its own adherents there is a
vast difference of opinion as to what constitutes a " reasonable want."   For everybody knows, that its most prominent leaders, form an aristocracy whose every-day wants
and habits differ widely from those of their followers.
Marx and Lasalle, for example, stood far above the poor

laboring-men; not only on account of their education, but
also on account of their social habits of life. Their in-
dignation against the lot of the poor working-class, proceeds from the softly-upholstered study. Dr. Aveling
and his Eleonore, during their recent visit to the United
States, even at the expense of the poor and needy workman, could not deny themselves the luxury of champagne
and the frequenting of theatres and the like. Indeed it
would be extremely amusing if it were not too criminally
serious to see Socialism leading its own subjects by the
nose.

Taken altogether we are driven to the conclusion that
Socialism completely fails in the most essential part of
its system—the distribution of the collective income—
to satisfy both reason and common sense. But as far as
this failure is studied, it must be considered a crime as it
holds out to the poor trodden-down working classes a
promise, that never can be fulfilled. Besides it betrays a
poor statesmanship on the part of the socialistic theorists
and leaders, when they keep up a constant agitation for
the overthrow of all existing economic order and forms
of government, without clearly and minutely exhibiting
the proposed social order, and the formation of the state
of the future. Thus far they leave it to their opponents
by way of reasoning and logical deductions to supply the
deficiency.

Finally allow me to remark that Socialism underrates the technical difficulties which the realization of its huge system would create.   The general opinion is that the future would regulate everything of itself.   Marx, for example, was a complete laisser-faire-man in this respect. But it requires certainly not much common sense, in order to see that such a world production on account of its immensity, would have to be systematized in its very minutiæ.   What a collosal apparatus would be necessary merely to supervise and control the whole.   If Socialism did not for the purpose of its infernal agitation suppress all considerations of that, and other kinds, it would at once give up the task as one not to be accomplished. Even if it should succeed in bringing about the projected upset, woe would be to the leaders on the morning after the bloody night of the social revolution, if they would or could not speedily satisfy the thousand-fold wishes which they had awakened, or could not realize the hopes of the multitudes called forth by their continued agitation; nay, if they should not fulfill the phantastic expectations, cherished by the misled mass.   Even if the ideal state of the future should safely pass these first cliffs, the technical supervision of such a huge production would offer to the everlastingly critical and sovereign socialistic people so many sides for an attack, that tinder for new social revolutions would constantly accumulate.   Of course all these doubts and fears have no weight with the Socialists, as most of them maintain with Fourier that: " A change of the organization of economy, would raise nature to an astounding and inexhaustible fruitfulness and human character to an unheard-of peaceableness and harmony of volition." But experience of thousands of years gone by, confirms our conviction, that the ushering in of the expected millennium is dependent on other than mere economical conditions and forces.

Summing up the result of our criticism, we met in Socialism a system that rests on an un-Christian, irreligious, atheistic basis and which for that very reason directs its destructive work against religion, as well as against the organized church; against the state, as well as against society ; against marriage, as well as against the family ; against capital, as well as against property, and individual liberty. Its principles as interpreted by it are visionary, and their carrying into effect impossible.

Now, here the question arises : Why should we trouble ourselves at all about a scheme that is, at least in its economic aspect, so utopian, vague, impracticable and delusive? Why should we not leave it to its own doom, with the expectation that it will of itself explode, or crumble into dust? The answer to these inquiries lies in the fact so often overlooked, that Socialism is pre-eminently a religious or rather irreligious system. Were it not for its atheistic attitude it would, I venture to say, have died out long ago. But atheistic materialism gives life, energy and nerve to it. And it is this irreligious position, that by the force of logical conclusion compels it to put itself in deadly opposition to all Divine or human, ecclesiastical or social and economic relations, orders, rules and arrangements which hitherto claimed to exist either by direct appointment of God, or by Divine permission. But it is also this infernal character that makes Socialism so extremely dangerous for all classes of society: for the church, because it has to encounter on every side the blasting influence of unbelief; for the state and society, because their very foundations are called into question, and for the poor laboring classes, because they are criminally deceived, and used as the available instruments to keep mankind in terror. Now this two-fold character of Socialism must also decide the position, which the church, the state and society in general has to take respectively, with reference to this alarming movement. But of that we will have something more to say in our next lecture.

LECTURE V.

THE SOLUTION OF THE SOCIAL QUESTION.

That there is such a thing as a social question agitating mankind at present, no one will deny. Not many years ago we in this country were not at all disturbed by it, while now it has spread through the length and breadth of the land, and assumed such a formidable character as to create uneasiness. And that under the exceptionable blessing of civil and religious liberty, and an unsurpassed national wealth. Certainly evidence enough that the present social commotion is of a general, deeply-seated and desperate nature. Neither is there a shadow of doubt that "all the revolutionary, destructive elements of Science, of Religion and of Politics are summoned by the social question to take active part in a decisive battle." (Lange.) Hence the great necessity and importance to approach the solution of this intricate problem with all energy and determination. There is at this time no other subject that demands a closer attention and a more united, persistent effort and speedy adjustment than this one.

But in order to be able to remove the difficulty it is absolutely necessary first of all to uncover and to lay bare the very source of the evil before any attempt is made to apply a successful remedy.

Now, it has been said, and we would not gainsay the assertion, that the economical conditions of the dependent classes are at present actually not any worse, in general, rather better than they were in times past. But it is thought that the wonderful advancement made in science, culture, refinement and the multiplied conveniencies of life has created a different conception of the social standard. Hence economic conditions are considered now as being oppressive and needing a reform which our forefathers found very agreeable. Demands are made at present on society and the body politic which the past would not have ventured to raise. The universal striving of the nations after a higher grade of culture is calling forth a higher degree of humanity, a keener sense of right, a loftier idea of national purpose, and a greater sensitiveness as to duty. But while this opinion presupposes a discrepancy between that which is and what ought to be, and while it explains to us the process by which this disagreement has come to be felt, it leaves us utterly in the dark as to how the acknowledged evil originated; neither can it on that account, suggest any effectual remedy.

Now, if our delineations of the system of Free Competition and of Socialism were correct, then the germs of the present social disturbances must be looked for in the fertile soil of Materialism, Rationalism and Atheism. The ethical materialism of the seventeenth and eighteenth centuries caused: 1. That *political* materialism which founded society, not on the everlasting rock of God's moral law, but on the "contrat social," on a legal contract—"a standpoint which forms the lowest grade that the State as well as science can occupy." 2. That *economic* rationalism which based the community not on the Divine law of love of one to the other, and the principle of common interest, but on the exchange and labor contract. The exclusive bond to hold together the atomized members of the commonwealth, is in either case *egotism*. Out of this materialistic rationalism naturally grew. 3. That *atheistic* socialism, which undertakes to place society entirely on the foundation of unbounded *sensuality*. And can we expect anything else from it? There is, indeed, logic in the language of a socialistic issue when it avers: "Whosoever takes away from the people Heaven, must give to them at least the earth. When in feudal times Hierarchy bent the necks of men, it offered to them anyhow a mild hope of another, of a better world. But the privileged classes of the present, what have they to offer to those millions by whose pining away, aggravated by toil and labor, they are enabled to enjoy the pleasures of life? You miserable Pharisees of the liberal Bourgoisie that have snatched away from the people the consolation of pious belief, where is your logic? The logic of the history of the world is severer than yours. We are done with Heaven. Now then, the people are justified in reclaiming from you the earth." (Kuntze, p. 95 f.)

These facts, sad as they are, must be acknowledged, if we ever expect to find a remedy for the spreading disease. In other words, society in general, high and low, poor and rich, employers and employed, those governing and those governed, must become convinced of the fact, which history has established again and again, that social and economic disturbances are invariably the result of a religious decline of the mass. Unless this conviction takes place, every effort to divert the social question of its alarming character will be in vain. On the other hand, when sin is recognized as lying at the bottom of the present uneasy state of affairs, then the proper remedy for a permanent cure of the existing evil will suggest itself. The Christian will at once see the necessity of introducing into all conditions of social and economic life, the

healing powers from on high.   And as the various preserving elements of society, of the state, the community and
the church by the revolutionary attitude of the present
movement are threatened alike with destruction of their
vital parts, and are materially checked in the discharge of
their respective duties, it rests upon them separately and
conjointly to put forth every effort, and to task all en-
ergies and available means to stay, if possible, the social
inundation.

In what manner each of these essential factors of society
ought to lay hands on the imperative reform, I will endeavor briefly to specify.   ·

I. THE DUTY OF THE STATE.

In a time in which innumerable infernal powers are at
work to undermine the very foundations of all social, civil
and religious orders, it is of the highest importance that
the State as such should keep in mind its historic origin
that is, its *Christian* character.   For it admits of no doubt
that this civil organism in its present form, be that monarchical or democratic, has been developed under and by
means of the power of the spirit of Christianity.   This
indubitable fact at once subjects each seperate government to a higher order and the laws thereof, and raises
Christianity to the authority of a standard by which legislation as well as administration is to be guided.   Not that
I should maintain that it was the purpose either of Chris-

tianity or of the State to furnish the body politic with a specifically *Christian* code of civil or social laws.   But I do hold that all legal regulations and measures in their motives as well as in their practical issues must reflect and actualize the eternal thoughts and principles of Divine justice and mercy as they are embodied and expressed in the Word of life.   Hence the State must allow the spirit of Christanity to influence its legislative and administrative actions, and must forever discard the maniac discovery and idea of the French revolution that the State had to be atheistic.

Having thus obtained a firm basis, the State will at once perceive the necessity of purging its legal statutes from the leaven of that *Roman* perception of right which especially since the naturalistic movement of the seventeenth and eighteenth centuries, has exercised a moulding influence on civil and even on ecclesiastical legislation of Christian nations.   It is true the Roman law on account of its complete arrangements and order, its nice juridical discriminations and distinctions has ever aroused the admiration of the civil world.   But as it entirely ignores the relation of the creature to an absolute Creator, of man to a Supreme Lawgiver—as it is merely based on perverted existing human relations, for that reason it lacks all those elements which, according to Scripture, make up the idea of real, substantial right.   In the eyes of the Word of

God, the heathen world does not know judgement (Isa.
xlii: 1; Ps. cxxvii: 19-20). Hence the Roman conception
of right ought in no way to define the civil, social and economic relations of those, who by virtue of their Christian
birth, education and covenant-relation are to be governed
by the higher law of their covenant God.

In what manner the State should carry out its direct
cultural work with special reference to the present social
and economic needs cannot be a matter of doubt. In the
first place it has to summon and cross-examine itself
whether and how far by legislative measures it has facilitated the one-sided formation of individualistic capitalism.
For we are convinced that the latter would never have
become such an oppressive power, if from the beginning
of the present ruling system the necessary legal restrictions had been issued and enforced. Legislation in the
past has too often shown itself very accommodating to the
demands of capitalism while it persistently has disregarded
the just claims and complaints of the working classes.
Thus, for example, in England " at the beginning of the
great revolution in industry and traffic, the suffering laborers had applied to the Legislature for redress. But it
had declared that it could not alter anything in the eternal
laws of nature, which governed the conditions of labor.
In consequence of that, the workmen had tried to help
themselves by demolishing factories and machines until

they were threatened with the penalty of death, and until about a dozen laborers were hung. Then followed the agitation for a legal restriction of the time of labor: but it required *thirty years* before sufficient provisions for the protection of women and children in factories could be obtained." (Brentano.) As a natural consequence we see one part of the English wage-earners turn to the doctrine of John Owen while the other fell in with the socialistic party of the Chartistic movement. Thus not only in England, but in other countries the civil powers, by acts of omission as well as by commission, have materially aided and are still furthering the formation of social extremes. These failures must be perceived and acknowledged before they can be rectified.

Again in our times of social commotion and anarchistic hankering after a thorough overthrow, the government is perfectly justified in making use of the repressive power with which it is endowed. But at the same time it would make a sad mistake, would it exclusively depend on that prerogative and right. On the contrary, now more than ever, the State has to show its readiness to solve the social question without resorting at once to extreme measures, or relying on its punitive, resentive power. The various governmental, administrative branches have themselves actively to enter into the mental contest waged in our days, and must put forth every effort to call in the different preserving and upbuilding elements within their boundaries, as church, school and family, in order to take part in the great work of bringing into harmonious co-operation all the social and economic factors of society. By doing this the threatening ruin, assuming constantly larger dimensions, will, and must be prevented. In this respect the Imperial modification of the necessity of an exceptional socialistic law for Germany strikes the key-note, when it considers the repressive means merely as " pre-conditions for the cure of the evil, not as the cure itself," and when it further says: " The active co-operation of all the preserving elements of civil society is necessary in order, by a reviving of religion, by enlightening and instruction, by fortifying the sense for right and morals as well as by further economic reforms, to pluck out the roots of the evil."

Above all, the State has to perceive its duty in the direction of a just economic legislation. Here as yet a wide and fruitful field opens itself to its activity. Unfortunately, as was intimated before, legislation has yielded too much to the influence of the School of Smith and Ricardo, ,and for that reason has concerned itself too eagerly about the advantages of producing capital while it neglected the interests of producing labor. But the national life of any people will not develop itself peacefully and prosperously, unless these two indispensable factors of human life and happiness are made the objects of legislative impartiality, so that they share proportion-ately in the increase. Now, former as well as present statistics prove beyond a doubt that everywhere national income has advanced, while individual gain has not kept equal step with the former. The entire economic progress of our time, however, is of such a kind that there exists the possibility to raise the working classes in their mater-ial and cultural conditions, without being in the least compelled to injure or deprive any of the possessing classes. Here then, the State has to begin its activity by advising ways and means that will actualize the extant possibility. If the ruling industrial system is unwilling to co-operate in the solution of the economic problem, then the State is under solemn obligation by its interven-tion to bring about a correction. This can be done in a twofold manner: 1. By restricting the power of private capital and the contents of contracts made, if both of these individual privileges are becoming instruments for the oppression of the working classes.

When, for example, capitalism makes use of the right of *migration* merely for the purpose of collecting wage-earn-ers en masse in a particular place in order to forgo the just demands of the laboring forces then and there extant, then it becomes the State, by some legislative measures to throw obstacles in the way of exercising that right. Or, when the employment of women and children in factories evidently is invited only for the purpose of dispensing with the more costly male-hands, then the welfare of the family as well as that of the community demands that such ruinous tactics by means of more stringent factory-laws be made impossible, at least be reduced to the smallest possible number of exceptions. For the State on account of its position and object, is bound to interfere "Wherever interests are at stake which from their very nature are unable to protect themselves, or where those, to whom naturally the defense thereof is intrusted, consider it an advantage to exercise this guardianship either not at all, or insufficiently. But children cannot protect themselves and parents very often are tempted, for the sake of worldly gain to sacrifice their own off-spring, while the entire State has a lively interest in the bodily, mental and moral integrity of all its subjects." (Haspe.) Especially does this duty of interfering become imperative, "when even the working of wife and child is insufficient to furnish to the entire family the necessary food and rest, and thus not only a single individual is sacrificed, but that entire vital organism pines away and decomposes which is the foundation of the State." (Truempelmann.)

It is true, at present, the social legislation of all civilized countries manifests the willingness to rectify the glaring economic evils, and in consequence of that, wholesome improvements have been made of late. But the work of adjusting the labor troubles has merely begun— there is obviously time and opportunity enough for more legislative activity in this very respect.

2. In some cases the State will have to take certain branches of economic pursuit out of the hands of private management and bring the same under its own control, if it ever intends to break the intolerable power of the one-sided development of private undertakings. In some instances this has been done on the part of the State with the greatest success, as, for example, in the management of all postal affairs, the taking charge of the means of public instruction, of public highways, etc., and in some countries even in the assumption of telegraph and railroad service. But it ought to be done also with all such *monopolies* which have become or are becoming an oppression to an entire nation or a great part thereof. Besides, there are such branches of industry that are notoriously and decidedly deleterious to human health; such ought never to be permitted to become the objects of private speculation, unless strictly guarded by legal regulations and oversight.

When the Government of any country thus becomes itself an economic power, then it enters into competition with private pursuits and exercises a wholesome and checking influence on the same.

Again, as the question of *wages* confessedly forms the most essential part of the social problem, the State cannot pass it by, but has to make it an object of its legislative concern. It is by no means advisable to leave this salient point any longer to the self-regulation of Manchesterism, if that question shall not be made still more intricate and complicated than it has become already by socialistic imbroglios. The ruling system of Free competition, as we have convinced ourselves, has shown itself utterly incapable of creating a satisfactory relation between capital and labor. Nay more, "our present laws respecting possessions do not purpose to satisfy fully all wants according to the measure of extant means. Our Codes of laws touching private rights, do not contain one single legal sentence that would direct to the individual those goods and services that are necessary for the maintenance of his existence." (Menger, p. 3.) The economic system of Smith as well as legislation, influenced by that system, occupies in this respect the position which Malthus with reference to individual right somewhat brutally but pertinently expresses in the well-known words: "A man who is born into a world already possessed, if he cannot get subsistance from his parents on whom he has a just demand, and if the society do not want his labor, has no claim of right to the smallest portion of food, and, in fact, has no business to be where he

is. At nature's mighty feast there is no vacant cover
for him. She tells him, be gone, and will quickly execute
her own orders." (An essay on the principle of population, 2nd ed. 1803, p. 531.)

But if anything is certain, it is the fact that Socialism
will always find a cause to revolutionize the masses, as
long as the flagrant disproportion between capital and the
remuneration of labor will last. As, however, according
to all past experience, the possessing and ruling classes,
out of their own accord will not take steps to arrange this
economic relation more justly, the welfare of the community demands that the State should manifest its influence in the direction of the solution of the alarming
problem. Self-evidently it is not a part of its function
to fix a scale of wages for each individual branch of industry, or to command a normal working-day for the
different trades. But it cannot be questioned that it is
within the power of the Government to exercise a lasting
and restraining influence on the tendency of capitalism to
lower the standard of wages, if it will initiate measures as
have been mentioned, if it will grant a sufficient salary to
those in its own employ, and if it insists upon a thorough,
comprehensive and enforced Enquete with reference to
the movements of privately managed enterprises, in order
to shape its legislative steps accordingly. Every body-
politic that directs its exertions to the adjustment of the

claims of a righteous distribution of the proceeds of labor, takes hold of the evil by its roots, and adds immensely to its final removal.

Furthermore, it is the imperative duty of the State, with all available means, to put an end to the fearful devastation which capitalism is working " on the physical, mental and moral forces of the cultural foundations of society." Even the latest scientific researches confirm the former lamentable result, that individualistic capitalism, in its unrestrained development, has forever been gnawing the vital marrow of each industrial portion of a community. Thus, for an example, it is universally observed, that in industrial regions the frequency of stillbirths is greater than in purely rural districts. An offspring in such centers which is permitted to see the light, is by far more exposed to a premature death, than the children of other places. It is especially that rachitic English disease of children, which decimates the littleones in industrial regions. But this evil always has its origin in insufficient *nutriment* of the generators as well as of the generated. Very truly, therefore, says the celebrated *Dr. Singer*, that against this evil no medical remedies prevail anything, but that the butcher shop will.

With regard to the mental status in such manufacturing centers, the same sad observations are made. Generally common school education does not stand comparison with that of other places, not even with rural districts, where schooling has to contend with local difficulties. And as for the ethical and moral conditions of industrial regions,the unanimous testimony of recent moral-statisticians, as of Oettingen,Drobisch and others, is not at all in their favor.

Now, wherever such physical, mental and moral injuries are directly due to the deleterious expansion of the power of Capitalism, is it not the imperative duty of legislation, by means of sanitary, cultural and provident provisions to correct the evil ? Without any doubt. Many a State, indeed, has pursued a self-destructing policy by allowing capitalism, altogether too long, to draw upon the life-blood of its constituent parts. It is true, and we may thank God for it, in our days the necessity of looking after the physical and moral welfare of the dependent classes receives an attention on the part of statesmen, as it has never done before. But let no one for a moment suppose that everything in that direction was done what ought to be done. There is, above all, that most essential element of the economic and civil life of a nation, *the family*, that must become more the object of legislative care and concern. Unfortunately past legislation has too often favored private capital and national wealth at the expense of the poverty of the working families. This policy the State has to discard forever. For it is the family that forms the firm foundation of the social and civil organism of the body-politic. And it is also the family, where the present economic evil has its vital germ. Hence it is of the greatest importance that this essential, indispensable factor of society and State should be strengthened, protected and rendered secure against decay.

Finally, the State has to make every exertion to preserve another of its principal supports intact, namely, those *agraric* conditions, which are so essential to its development. They form at present for the State a sure foundation. Radical Socialism is aware of this fact only too well; consequently its open confession, that it was comparatively easy to begin a social revolution, but impossible to carry it through without the co-operation of the country people. Hence its indefatigable efforts to instill its abstruse ideas into the minds of the rural population, and on that account its constant success in such countries where, as in England, Ireland and Germany, the agraric conditions have been very oppressive. For this reason the State ought energetically to further the interests of agriculture, especially to protect the same against any overbearing of industrialism and mercantilism as well as against the rapacity of private speculation. It is by no means necessary, nor would it be wise to expropriate the owners of the soil, or to introduce communistic production, nor to nationalize the land. But one thing is

indispensably necessary : In the interest of the fer-
tility of the soil as well as of the welfare of the individual and the commonwealth, land must be kept out of
the clutches of private speculation.   Immense complexes
of ground in the hands of a few individuals have always
proved a curse to the community.   When one half of the
province of Africa, according to Pliny Hist. Nat. xviii: 35,
was found in the possession of but six men, then the
Roman Empire had approached its last stage of development.   Old Italy was ruined by its " Latifundia," and
England's and Ireland's scourge to day is the distortion of
their agraric conditions.   Lord *Beaconsfield*, a few years
ago did not betray much of Statesmanship, when in a
public address he gave to the English Latifundia-system
the preference over the French parcelling system.   Bad
as the latter is, in a social and economic aspect it is by
all means preferable to a state of things, as the agricultural conditions in the countries mentioned exhibit.   But
we pass on to the redress which is to be rendered in

THE ECONOMIC SPHERE.

Even the best intentions and exertions on the part of
the State will finally prove a failure, if the human factors
of production remain unwilling to co-operate in the solution of the social question.   The State cannot enforce a
reform, it needs the active help of the parties immediately
concerned and interested in such reform.   But here we

meet on the one side the possessing classes or the *capitalists*, on the other hand the *wage-earners*—the employers and the employed. Now, both of these must resolve in a candid Christian spirit to settle their differences.

As for the capitalists our historic investigation has convinced us that for the greatest part they have caused the social problem to assume such an alarming character. Hence society has a right to expect of them, not only not to oppose any longer such efforts that are made for the removal of existing economic evils, but also actively to devise ways and means for such a rectification. It is in their own interest as well as in that of society in general that they should make every effort to check the destructive forces of the day, and to initiate a peaceful and harmonious development of all social and economic elements.

Now, you will recollect that the mistakes of liberal economism previously mentioned, were due to erroneous conceptions. For this reason, political economy will have to consent to a rectification of these false, untainable ideas, and thus bring about a reform of its very foundation. And here first of all mention must be made of the fallacious opinion in regard to private capital and productive property, as it has been exposed in our critique of the system of free competition. The producing classes have to trace these categories to their proper origin, that is they must come to the conviction that property in capital and land, considered as a human institution, owes its existence merely to regards for social expediency. Consequently it cannot claim to be an unchangeable, irrevocable institute of right and economic development. Such a persuasion then will exercise a wholesome influence in various directions. In the first place the *right* to private capital possessions will not any longer be considered as an *absolute* one, but rather as a right granted to the individual because the exercise thereof in that form is considered by society as being mostly advantageous to the welfare of all. For this reason a right of absolute disposal is out of question. The obtaining of productive capital, even from a purely economic standpoint considered, involves the obligation to apply the same also in the interest of the whole community. Otherwise the very idea of private property is annulled. Adding to this those responsibilities which grow out of the religious relation between employers and employed, then we demand of the capitalistic powers that they free the system of unrestrained competition from its rationalistic embrace and place it on a Christian basis. The egotistic self-interest, this only impelling motive of the liberal method of production, has to give room to that spirit which expresses itself in the Apostolic words of admonition: " Not looking each of you to his own things, but each of you also to the things of others." Phil. ii: 4.

When in this manner political economy has received a sound moral basis, then *labor*, this indispensable factor in the creation of wealth, will receive that valuation which is due to it. In our treatise on the system of free competition we considered it as a principal error of physiocratic individualism that it looks upon human labor merely as upon a *mechanical* activity, which in the introduction of the division of labor is put on an equal footing with the technical achievement of *machinery*, and which on that account is only remunerated in so far as it is indispensable in the process of production. Manchesterism especially, in its extreme development has always failed to appreciate the fact that mere expenditure of force does by no means form labor, even when it is directed to a productive end. Human labor is rather a *personal* activity which on the one side *consciously* is turned toward the purposes of production, and which on the other hand allows itself as a serviceable achievement to be inserted into the systematized activity of the totality, in order not only to advance its own but also the common interests of society. That is, labor has a *personal*, a *social*, and an *ethical* character, and these three moments elevate it far above every mechanical movement, no matter how artful or efficient it may be. This fact capitalists have to acknowledge, they must consider human labor as a moral factor in the process of production, whose value is not to be measured

merely by a technical rule.   It is true, the present general-
enterprising in industry cannot desist from the accustomed *division of labor*, but that ought not to be allowed
to press down the personality of the wage-earner on a level
with machinery.   The workmen of the present day are by
far too conscious of their relative value and importance
in the economic process, as that they should acquiesce in
a persistent, intentional disregard of the industrial signification of labor.   They require, and justly so, the establishment of a more righteous relation of capital to labor,
or in other words, they demand of the employers a regulation of the wage question that will give labor its due
position and honor.   And there is one thing certain, if
the social question is ever to be solved, at least if it is to
loose its present threatening feature, then capital must
accede to an equitable settlement of the wage trouble.
When, for example, the technical improvements in industry render the production of goods more facile and efficient,—is there any reason why capital alone should
claim for itself the advantage and benefit of such facility;
and why it should leave wages on their former basis ?
Certainly, none.   Besides, it is not only a postulate of
humanity, but of *justice*, also, that while the production of
goods is constantly increasing, the working classes should
be enabled to better their condition also, so that they
find opportunity to participate in the higher gifts of cul-

ture, education and comfort. Rodbertus, indeed, does not demand anything unjust or unreasonable when he requests "not a more proper and equal division of the *means* of production, but rather a more just distribution of the *products* or proceeds of the goods." If that would be granted, then also the relation of production to *consumption* would be brought into a better harmony. As long as the consumptive inability or, in other words, the poverty of the masses remains the same, even while the production of the goods constantly advances, stagnations in trade must of necessity take place and become, as they have done, a scourge to modern society. Thus the increase in national wealth does not bring any amelioration to the greatest part of the people; on the contrary, causes and aggravates the economic extremes of rich and poor, threatens the social structure with destruction and undermines the foundation of civil government.

In view of these facts the possessing classes ought no longer to shrink from the fulfillment of their imperative duty to honor adequately human labor, if they do not mean to endanger their own well-being as well as the security of society.

In what manner and to what extent this advance in wages is to be made, is a matter of mutual agreement, as no fixed rule can be applied to each and every individual case. The manifoldness in the economic and local con-

.ditions of society, requires also a diversity in the arrangement and the method of compensating labor rendered. But one thing seems to be well established,
namely, that the system of *Co-partnership*, or of a *Tan-
tieme*, has worked to the great satisfaction of all parties
concerned. This method, slightly altered, was in vogue
already from the fourteenth to the seventeenth century.
In late years it has been introduced with great success,
not only in farming, but also in various branches of industry. The wage-earner, besides a fixed amount of
wages, receives also a previously announced pro-rata portion of the final net-profit of the business. Thus he actually becomes a partner in the concern, and this consciousness generally works well on both sides. The employer, in granting such a proportionate participation in
the proceeds, performs a moral act which secures to him
greater confidence on the part of his employees, and removes from him the odious stigma of an egotistic capitalist. The workmen, on the other hand, find it in their
own interest to work as much, as carefully and savingly
as possible. For every increase of the final gain secures
to them a larger share in the same. Besides, it has been
found that under such an arrangement the laborers themselves exercise a mutual supervision, and thus the productive ability is materially enhanced all around. Wherever
this system has been introduced in England, Germany and

our own country, the results have been advantageous for both parties. In spite of the additional compensation thus granted to the workmen, the employers have gained a larger profit than they had been able to realize before such an arrangement was made. The reason for this lies in the fact that they had it in their power to secure more trustworthy and able hands, and by means of harmonious feelings to keep off the damaging consequences of destructive strikes, and similar conjunctures.

Whether such an agreement could be introduced into every branch of industry, is a question that cannot be answered at once in the affirmative. But wherever it is made, two things are absolutely necessary for its final success. The owner of the business has to make the pro-rata division of the net-income conscientiously, so as to tally with his voluntary stipulation and with the figures on his books. The workmen, on the other hand, have to be very careful not to over-rate the announced net result, nor to underrate the working expenses, two points on which laborers in general are very skeptical and distrustful. In other words, the Christian spirit of honesty, candor and mutual confidence has to penetrate even such a beneficial system, if it is expected to last, and to prove a blessing to the economic, moral and religious welfare of society.

Where, however, the system of co-partnership, for

some reasons cannot be considered, there are, undoubtedly, other ways and means by which capitalists have it
in their power to bring about a more satisfactory relation
between themselves and their employees. There are, for
an illustration, according to well-authenticated reports,
some mauufacturers who increase the wages of the men
under their charge, as they advance in years, especially
so from the time of their getting married, without asking
any additional work of them. By so doing they enable
the head of the family to support the same without being
compelled to send wife and children out to earn a mere
pittance. Others are endeavoring to enhance the material, mental and moral well-being of those depending on
them, by founding, supervising and aiding various institutions for the mutual insurance of the workmen, by sup-
plying healthy and comfortable dwelling-apartments, or
by building churches, schools, libraries and reading-
rooms for those intrusted to their care. All these and
similar beneficent provisions are of incalculable influence
in the solution of the social problem. Besides, thus far
each benevolent, philanthropic capitalist has found it to
be in his own interest when he conducts his business on
strictly Christian principles. He has preserved to himself a good conscience and kept clear of the reproach of
having obtained his wealth out of the sweat of the brow
of his workmen.

As long as in economy the two factors, employer and employed, or capitalists and wage-earners are indispensable, so long it will be of the greatest importance to regulate the relation between the two in a just and harmonious manner. And as wages or *money*, by general consent and custom, has become that instrument by which this relation is maintained and expressed, it is a matter of grave consequence to fix this economic ligature in such a manner, that the one part of the mutual relation is not encroached upon by the other. Otherwise there will be no concert of feelings nor of action. Hence even the self-interest of capitalists demands that they should determine the scale of wages on a sound and fair basis. It is true, money is and remains but a cold, lifeless metal, which only then will produce vital heat when it is made to flow by the power of the Christian motive of well-wishing and love to the neighbor. The employer, therefore, should rather offer an advance in wages than wait until a prospect of material loss compels him to it. General experience confirms the assertion that a self-prompted concession always creates a more satisfactory relation than power and coercion.

In short, the duty of the employer does not end there and then, when he has fulfilled his obligations as far as they have been imposed upon him by a juridical contract between him and his workmen. His relation to them is withal a moral one, and on that account he is bound to a conscientious regulation of the wage interest and to the furtherance of the social, mental and moral conditions of his laborers.   It is, indeed, high time that the Cainitic sentiment: " Am I my brother's keeper?" should make room in the hearts of the capitalists to that spirit that considers also the dependent, poor wage-earner a brother.

Passing on to the co-operation of the *working-classes* it will be seen at once that they are too an essential factor in the industrial process, as that their behavior in the present social excitement should be unimportant.   On the contrary, to a great extent, it will depend upon them whether society is to be shaken to its very foundation, or not.   The following suggestions are intended as hints in what direction the laborer has to conceive his obligations.

At the present time, when social excitement waxes hot, and agitation becomes impassionate, the wage-earners cannot be admonished too impressively to preserve cool ' blood, to advance with sobriety and prudence and above all to resist every attempt to urge them to acts of violence.   While nobody justly can deny to them the right to *coalition*, in order to consolidate their interests, or of expressing to their employers fairly and squarely their grievances, every well-minded person will and must dissuade them from all measures as well as from all connections that aim a blow at the existing order of society. The poor laborer by no means advances his own interest, nor that of his fellow-workmen, when he unites with those who on account of their athestic ruin have lost every regard for Divine or human orders.

Moreover, as liberalistic economism as well as Socialism have caused a great confusion in economic conceptions, it is of vital importance that the laborer also should learn to understand the actual *value and signification* of labor in itself, and in its relation to the other factors of production. By means of such a correct knowledge he will be enabled to apply the right rule to all the productive elements, and will avoid those mistakes so commonly made by wage earners. Then, for an instance, he will consider his daily work not only a burden, the rendering of a sacrifice, but as a moral vocation given to him by the will of his God for the purpose of conscientiously advancing his own and the interest of his fellow-men in their temporal as well as in their spiritual relations. Wherever labor is rendered in this way, there wages, this lifeless metal, will not be regarded as the only and exclusive equivalent for exertions made, but there also the moral consciousness of having accomplished something for the promotion of the general welfare, and of having fulfilled a higher calling, will be taken into account.

Besides, the proper conception of labor prevents that one-sided undervaluation of the relation of capital to work, as it is found in and propagated by the socialistic system. Formerly labor was degraded and enslaved, at present there is the opposite danger, that of giving undue superiority and weight to mere *manual* rendering, when compared with mental exertions, or with the claims of working capital. But, when the mind of the wage earner is set right as to the proper signification of labor he will at once see the necessity of a gradation of the constituent parts of society, will perceive for the economic process the absolute indispensableness of enterprising capital as well as of producing labor. Such an employee will also readily recognize the responsibility, risks, cares and anxieties of the capitalist, will, therefore, willingly concede to capital its proportionate claim to the proceeds of production. In other words, when employers as well as employed mutually endeavor by means of the Christian principles of justice and well-meaning to agree upon the proper relation of capital to labor, the question as to the just distribution of the net income will regulate itself. At least the social tension will loose that unpleasant, alarming feature which characterizes it at present. Of course, we cannot expect such a reciprocal recognition of mutual responsibilities, rights and claims, unless both employer and employed have learned to become one in a unit higher than mere material interest—in the love of Christ.

Now, a word or two in regard to *Unions, Strikes*, etc.

"The workmen," says Contze, "have the right, they even owe it to themselves, their families, their co-workers and to society in general, to organize themselves in order to prevent their being wasted in the interest of capital or capitalists. They are justified, when, for that purpose, they claim the political influence due them. They are right when they come in for a proper share in education and all legitimate enjoyments of life, etc." Now, such trade-unions and co-operative associations have existed at all times. The recent immense progress of industry has materially favored the formation of such economic fraternities. They have indeed become a power, which capital can no longer ignore or set aside. Neither can it be denied that they have been of great value and advantage wherever they were conducted with circumspection, rigid dicipline and to a proper end. Such associations counteract the atomizing tendency of the present economic society and the anarchy of free competition, besides exercising a salutary influence on their members by awakening a feeling of common interest— l'esprit du corps.

But when many of the trade-unions represent merely *organized* and *armed labor*, which thus is considered better qualified to wage the contest with capital; when associations are formed for the sole purpose of furthering self-interest, without any regard to the welfare of the community; when they allow themselves to be towed by party politics or even by the social democracy; when they attempt to exercise a terrorism, not only over their own members but also over capital; when they bind the con-sciences of their subjects with an iron-clad oath to obey the dictates of their leaders; when they tresspass on the sacred ground of individual liberty; then symptoms present themselves to us which are by no means calculated to inspire us with the hope of a speedy solution of the social problem.

As for *Strikes*, *Tie-ups*, *Lock-outs* and other anomalies, they may at present be considered as necessary tactics in the mutual conflict, in order to gain a temporary advantage. Or they may be regarded on the part of Socialism as the best means to drive society into a state of anarchy. But every person of sober judgment no matter whether capitalist or laborer, ought by this time to be convinced of the fact that such coercive measures will never conduce to a harmonious development of common interests. They are constantly widening the chasm and inflaming the bitterness.

FINALLY AS TO THE DUTY OF THE CHURCH.

That under the present emergency a solemn obligation rests with the Church of the Lord Jesus Christ, only ignorance and selfishness can deny. But in speaking of the Church, we refer principally to the Evangelical portion

thereof. For it is a well-known fact that the Catholic
Church long ago has initiated measures to counteract the
subversive influences of the present social commotions,
and, if possible, to turn them to her own advantage. And
what is still more important, we have to face the humiliat-
ing truth that the ranks of Socialism and Anarchism are
mostly swelled by former members of the Protestant persuasion. This sad fact ought to induce the Evangelical
Church, above all the others, to awaken to a sense of her
duty, and to strain every nerve to counter-influence the
growing evil. But in order to be fitted for such an important work, it is absolutely necessary that the evil should
be discerned and traced to its proper source. The fountain head of the turbid stream has to be discovered before
the healing tree can be applied. Even if such a thorough
research should render our long cherished ideas, as to the
cause of the labor troubles utterly untainable, it has to be
made, notwithstanding.

Now, if in our previous expositions we were not entirely
mistaken, then the social and socialistic evils of the present day are a disease, which under constantly growing
oppressive circumstances has developed itself, until it has
assumed the alarming character of an epidemic which
threatens the existing order of Church, State and Society
with destruction. The germs of this contagion we discovered in a general religious declining of the masses,

and in a continually spreading of materialistic Mammonism. This truth has to be acknowledged and fearlessly
to be stated. Each individual, whether poor or rich,
whether capitalist or wage earner, has to be told that the
sins of the masses have brought about the massive misery.
That is, each economic person ought to put to him or herself
the serious question: How far have I, by sinful deeds of
omission and commission, added to the general decline of
religion and of social disharmony. From this heart-search-
ing self-examination the Church can in no wise exclude
herself, for the judgement of God always " begins at the
Sanctuary." She, above all, has to inquire in all earnestness, whether directly or indirectly she has not advanced
the one-sided developement of the power of Capitalism, by
allowing, even in her own midst, to capital and station in
life an undue influence and precedence, and by not hold-
ing up at all times to Mammonism its injustice. On the
other hand, the sad position of the laborer in the present
commotion, especially the fact that the great mass of the
poor working class have become estranged from the
Church, ought to cause her seriously to reflect whether
she has always made just that dependent class of society
the special object of tender care and watchfulness, which
according to the illustrious example of the great Head of
the Church ánd the explicit command of the word of Life,
it is entitled to.

Having thus laid a solid foundation in humiliation, the Church is able to proceed to the solution of the troublesome problem.

Now, our former considerations have convinced us that neither cold-hearted capitalism, nor radical atheistic Socialism is capable of bringing about a harmonious state of affairs. The help must come from the Church and from her alone. For, neither the State as such, nor the employer, nor the workman will be in a condition to deal out justice, equity and forbearance, unless all of these elements of human society are governed and filled by the spirit of Christian love and consideration. But who, aside from the Church, will put forth efforts to permeate the different social ranks and orders with the power of Christ and Christianity? To the Church, therefore, falls the all-important task to apply to the present sores of society the healing balm of the Gospel of redeeming love and condescension.

But especial emergencies require special efforts. Allow me to particularize some of such specific endeavors. It admits of no controversy that the Gospel of our Master is pre-eminently the Glad Tidings for the poor of this world, for the down-trodden and disinherited; while, on the other hand, it unsparingly condemns Capitalism, Mammonism and Egotism. Now, let at this time of social fermentation and commotion, this truth stand out in bold

relief over every pulpit in the land, in every church-
paper, and in all the proceedings of ecclesiastical bodies.
Nay, more, as the great mass of the wage earners as well
as of the unchristian capitalists are not reached by the
usual Church agencies, *special efforts* have to be made to
disseminate the truth of the Gospel also in its social bear-
ings, among the rich and the poor, the employers and the
employed.   If at any time, it is at present the imperative
duty of the Church, speedily to carry out her Master's
command: "Go out quickly into the streets and lanes
(and we venture to add: into the counting-rooms) of the
city and bring in hither the poor, and the maimed, and
the halt, and the blind." Luke xiv:21.   The capitalist
has to be told that he is the Lord's steward, responsible
not only for the application of his means but also for his
dealings with those that are dependent on him.   The
laboring class must be convinced, that it is an utterly unfounded and malicious charge on the part of some dema-
goguic leaders, that Christianity was exclusively a religion for the rich, and that the Clergy and the Church—
the Church of the lowly and hard working Jesus of
Nazareth!—stood with their sympathies on the side of
cold-hearted capitalism.   And do not let us for a moment
suppose that, because a man is a heartless capitalist, that
on that account he is beyond the reach of Divine grace.
Or, because so many of the deluded laborers have allowed

themselves to be enrolled in socialistic and anarchistic ranks and files, that for this reason they are but the object of police surveillance. There are to-day men engaged in the Berlin city missions, who but a few years ago, preached lawlessness, uproar and destruction. The Lord's "portion is with the great and he shall divide the spoil with the strong." Isa. 53.

But this is not all. Our time is peculiarly a time of *organizations.* Since the rising of the unjust power of capital, labor has endeavored, by means of trades-unions and secret societies to check this overpowering influence. The alarming energy of Socialism lies in its well-disciplined international—yea infernal—organism. Of what nature this formation is, we have seen before. And as for the first-mentioned fraternities it is an open secret that many, if not the most of them, are unchristian or even antichristian in their principles, motives and purposes. Now, is there any reason why the devil should always have the longest end of the rope? Certainly not. Why then should not Christian ministers and layman, Christian employers and employees, without reference to creed or ecclesiastical color, unite, in order to stand as a healing power between capitalism on the one, and revolutionary, unchristianizing schemes on the other hand? When the first Christian Church in Jerusalem was disquieted by a social economic trouble, the Apostles did not act on the

Manchester idea that the evil of murmuring would rectify itself, neither did they tell those neglected Grecian widows that they better patiently submit to the wrong. No, they at once organized a Board of Deacons, or Elders, as some will have it, in order to prevent any recurrence of the same kind.

Now, the church of God as well as society is at present fearfully disquieted and injured by social disturbances. Why then, should not the Christians of the land unite in one common effort to create, if possible, a better feeling between the rich and the poor, to bring about a more just relation of capital to labor, and thus reclaim some who, for economic reasons and influences have been lost to the Church and to their God! When the realm of darkness is marshaling its forces into line, certainly the church of God cannot look on the heart-rending devastations, perpetrated on precious human souls, without rallying her blood-bought members around the cross of her crucified Redeemer, and from there send them out into the highways of life, for the purpose of rescuing the multitudes from final destruction.

In conclusion, let every professor of Christianity by the power of God's infinite grace banish from his own heart and life every unrighteousness and selfishness. The glaring inconsistency of many a so-called Church-member has increased the bitterness of the masses against the

Word of Life, and robbed them of the last remnant of confidence in the Church and her saving work. If we intend at all to do something for the welfare of others, either bodily, socially, economically or spiritually, the unselfish, self-denying love of Christ must shine forth from our words as well as from our dealings with our fellowmen. And, in whatever human relation of life that Divine power and love prevails, there is no room for a disturbing social question.

www.ingramcontent.com/pod-product-compliance
Lightning Source LLC
Chambersburg PA
CBHW030835270326
41928CB00007B/1065